W9-CET-032

The Cooperative
THINK TANK

Graphic Organizers to Teach Thinking in the Cooperative Classroom

By
James Bellanca

IRI SkyLight
TRAINING AND PUBLISHING, INC.
Arlington Heights, Illinois

136716

The Cooperative Think Tank: Graphic Organizers to Teach Thinking in the Cooperative Classroom

Published by IRI/SkyLight Training and Publishing, Inc.
2626 S. Clearbrook Drive, Arlington Heights, Illinois 60005
800-348-4474, 847-290-6600
Fax 847-290-6609
info@iriskylight.com
http://www.iriskylight.com

Editors: Robin Fogarty, Carla Bellanca Kahler, Sharon Nowakowski
Type compositor: Donna Ramirez
Book designer and Typesetter: Bruce Leckie
Cover designer: David Stockman

© 1990 IRI/SkyLight Training and Publishing, Inc.
All Rights Reserved.

ISBN 0-932935-45-1
Printed in the United States of America.

0965G–5–98McN
Item Number 872

06 05 04 03 02 01 00 99 98   15 14 13 12 11 10 9 8 7

Contents

INTRODUCTION

A Word About Motivating Thinking by all Students

One of the most difficult challenges teachers face is motivating all children in the classroom to think and learn. Given 30 to 35 different learning styles, abilities, interests, attention spans and more, the task seems impossible.

In the lessons that follow, all pre-tested in a variety of classrooms, you will find sure-fire, reusable tools that have one central purpose: helping you motivate all your students to think more skillfully, to cooperate and to achieve, without burning yourself out. In each lesson two important components are incorporated:

1. A sound lesson design that includes:

    - **a clear learning objective**

    - **a visual set**

    - **demonstrations**

    - **clear instructions for guided practice, review and transfer**

    - **test suggestions**

2. Allowances for a variety of learning styles and abilities.

    A. Each lesson is built on a **specific visual organizer** that will enable students to see their thinking.

    B. Each lesson uses **cooperative learning strategies** and peer assistance structures to help students tutor and coach each other.

    C. Each lesson helps students **think about their thinking** (metacognition), move from the concrete to the abstract, and apply what they have learned to situations out of the classroom.

    D. Each lesson is a **high-involver**. It calls for each student to play with ideas, to explore and inquire in a climate that demands "no put-downs." To make this climate work, you play an important role. Here are ways you can help ensure active involvement by all students.

- **Set guidelines.** The DOVE guidelines are paramount.

  D = DEFER JUDGMENT! Do not use put-downs or make positive or negative judgments about others' ideas.

  O = OPT FOR OFF-BEAT! As a thinker, be different. Try different ways, seek a new combination.

  V = VAST NUMBERS ARE NEEDED! Go for quantity. From quantity comes quality.

  E = EXPAND! Piggyback or hitchhike on others' ideas.

- You make the cooperative group assignments. **Make different groups each time.** Mix, mix, mix. Break down cliques. Mix high and low achievers into groups of two or three.

- **Encourage everyone to contribute and share.** Don't let anyone dominate a group.

- **Encourage cooperation.** It will help groups if each student has a role: worrier, recorder/checker, encourager, etc.

  The *worrier's* job:
    Are we agreed on what to do?
    Are we doing what was asked?
    Is everyone helping?

  The *checker's* job:
    Have I written down everyone's ideas?
    Does everyone understand?
    Can everyone explain the answers?

  The *encourager's* job:
    "Good idea," "Let's go for it!" "Great job."
    Smile, give others thumbs up.

- **Structure united groups.** Use only one worksheet per group. Have the *checker* pre-test all members so that everyone can explain the group's chart. If your groups have high social skills, you can add a group grade for the product and the process.

- **If one or two don't want to work with a group, give them the option to do the task alone.** Experience shows that it won't be long before they want "in" with the group.

A Word About Cooperative Learning

Roger and David Johnson's research tells us there are five critical factors that make smoothly functioning cooperative groups. By combining the Johnsons' research with other findings and by adding another dimension, high thought, we have the following model in which the acronym BUILD (Marcus and McDonald, 1990) highlights the variables that produce the power in cooperative groups.

B = Build in higher-order thinking so students are challenged to think deeply and transfer subject matter.

U = Unite the class so students form bonds or trust which enable teamwork.

I = Individual learning: Each student is accountable for mastering all skills and knowledge. The groups are a means to facilitate mastery before the teacher checks each individual through quizzes, tests, essays or other more authentic assessment strategies.

L = Look back and debrief *what* and *how* students learned. Students are taught to "process" or "evaluate" their thinking, feelings and social skills. This emphasis on "taught" student evaluation shifts the responsibility for learning from the teacher to student.

D = Develop students' social skills. The teacher provides explicit training in the social skills. This helps students master cooperative skills and use those skills during cooperative work.

A Word About Grading and Evaluating

If you want to measure students' thinking, look at the products made by each group. For cooperation look for what the students do and say that shows cooperation. Where you can, avoid using grades with the lessons. Grades are a fast way to kill thinking in the classroom.

A Word About Transfer

These lessons are constructed to give you and the students high-involvement strategies for thinking together about what is being learned. In the initial lesson you should check for understanding. Help the students refine their thinking by using these visual tools.

Both you and they will benefit in future lessons if the tools are used over and over during the year. How many of the visual tools you introduce is up to you. Whichever you introduce, expect to use them over and over and over. You can concentrate on helping students use the tools after they have learned to master their basic content. Once students are skilled in the visual technique, give your regular tests and quizzes on content. You will see higher grades, increased involvement and more motivation.

Use the tools with easy topics, then bridge the skill into content. Check for understanding about content and method. Remember, the goal is to develop independent, self-directed learners who use the visual tools appropriately. This will require many practices throughout the year.

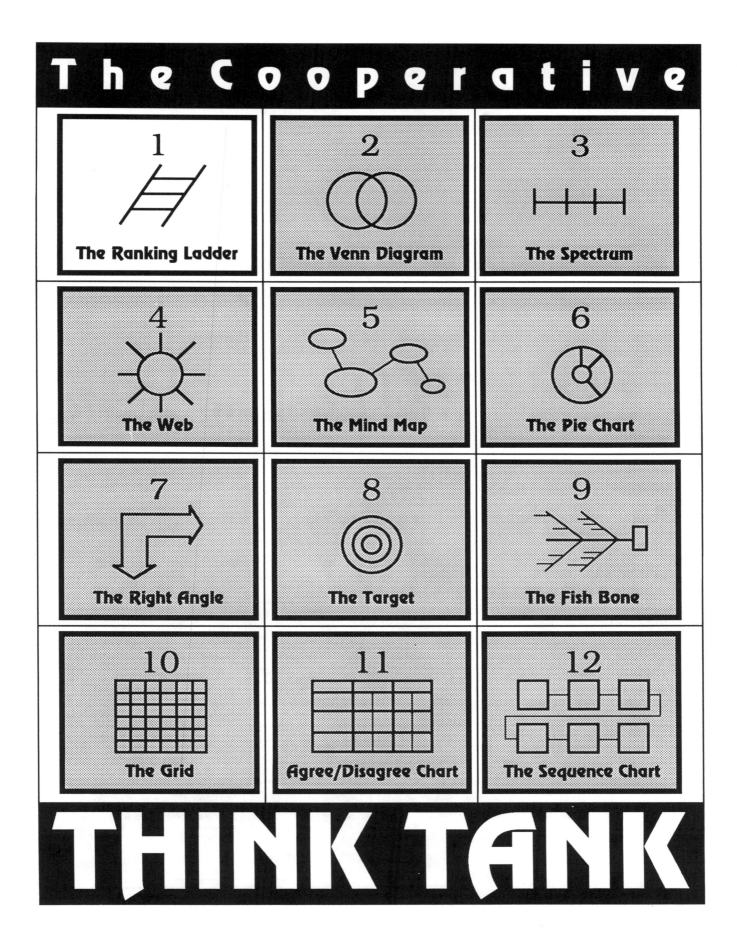

C H A P T E R

1

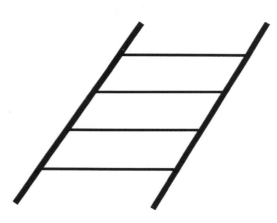

The Ranking Ladder

■ **PURPOSE**

To help students make rank orders.

■ **VOCABULARY**

Rank order: To rate, evaluate, weigh or judge in order of importance, value or size.

Criteria: Ways, standards or reasons by which we measure or decide a ranking.

■ **THINKING SKILL**

Evaluating

INTRODUCTORY LESSON

Draw a ladder on the board or overhead or show students a picture of a ladder. Ask students to give examples why ladders are used. List at least three answers on the board (e.g., climb, put out fire).

Ask a volunteer to come up to the board and "rank order" the answers. On the bottom rung, the student will copy the example that is most common (see ladder below). On the next rung, the second most common reason for using a ladder. Continue up the ladder until all the examples are placed in an order.

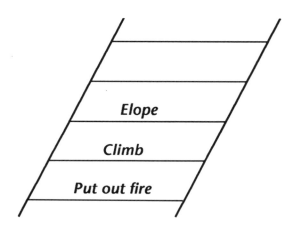

Ask if there are other ways to rank order uses of ladders. Ask the students to give reasons for their different arrangements. Instruct everyone to listen to everyone else.

Explain to the students that the steps of the ladder make a thinking tool that helps them see how they are ranking items. Explain the two vocabulary words, *ranking* and *criteria*.

Explain or ask for student examples of where else they might use a ranking ladder to see how important items are in relation to each other (i.e., their best subject in school, their biggest challenge, characters they most like or dislike in a story). Explain or discuss why it is important to give the reasons for the rank orders (thinking about thinking, clarifying choices).

Divide the students into mixed ability pairs. Assign a checker/recorder and a worrier.

Hand one copy of a ranking ladder to each pair. Each pair must agree on its rank orders and both partners must be able to explain the ranks.

ELEMENTARY SCHOOL SAMPLE

WHAT DOES A BEST FRIEND DO?
• helps in hard times
• sticks up for you
• does what you say
• tells you the truth

MIDDLE SCHOOL SAMPLE

WHAT IS THE BEST NEWS MEDIUM?
• TV
• newspaper
• magazine
• radio

SECONDARY SCHOOL SAMPLE

WHAT IS MOST IMPORTANT FOR SCHOOL SUCCESS?
• luck
• studying hard
• paying attention
• critical thinking

Check that all pairs know the ranking procedures with one sample list. Use the following example or one of your own:

1. Rank the following five items. Agree on your rankings and place them on the ladder.

   • Which do you like best? Spinach, oatmeal, rice, milk, apples.

2. Review the responses by randomly asking several recorders to explain their choices.

Give each pair a new ladder. Give the rankings that you have selected from your material (i.e., read a story and rank the characters according to their importance; rank historic figures from a social studies text according to their contributions; rank ways to solve a math problem). Give the criteria by which the student pairs will make their rankings (i.e., the bravest character, the easiest procedure; the most difficult steps).

After the ranks are done, randomly select a checker to explain the choices.

REVIEW & TRANSFER

Review or ask students to explain the key thinking processes necessary for ranking. After you have listed the ideas, rank them on the board. Use the ladder to show the first step, second step, etc.

YOUR IDEA FOR A RANKING

_____
_____
_____
_____
_____
_____
_____
_____

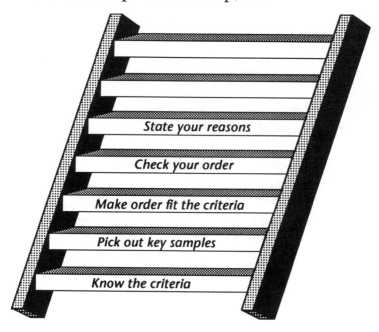

State your reasons

Check your order

Make order fit the criteria

Pick out key samples

Know the criteria

Now, assign student pairs to complete one or more practice rankings with other materials in your classroom. Check that they know the vocabulary, the ranking steps and how to explain why ranking is important as a thinking skill.

After you have held several in-class practices and given enough corrective feedback (accentuate the positive!) to see that all students can do and explain rank orders, give homework assignments from the textbook. Each assignment should require rank orders.

TEST

To test students' mastery of the ranking ladder:

- ☐ Have students define *rank order* and *criteria.*

- ☐ Have students select four concrete objects from their class work. Next, have them rank the items and explain their rankings.

- ☐ Have students select five concepts from their class work. Have students rank the items and explain their rankings.

- ☐ Have students list the five thinking steps used in making a rank order.

OPTIONAL

For more advanced practice, construct a rank ladder that applies to setting priorities in students' everyday encounters. What task or goal is more important to do first? second? etc? What is most important to do with the money they earn? and so on until they master the skill of rank ordering.

APPROPRIATE USE

- ■ To evaluate two, three, or more ideas, tasks, events, processes, characters, etc.

- ■ To prioritize steps or events in a process.

MIDDLE SCHOOL SAMPLE

WHAT IS THE MOST IMPORTANT INVENTION?
- **electric light**
- **telephone**
- **computer**
- **TV**
- **automobile**
- **airplane**

YOUR IDEA FOR A RANKING

_____

_____

_____

_____

_____

_____

_____

NAME _____   CLASS _____

RANKING LADDER

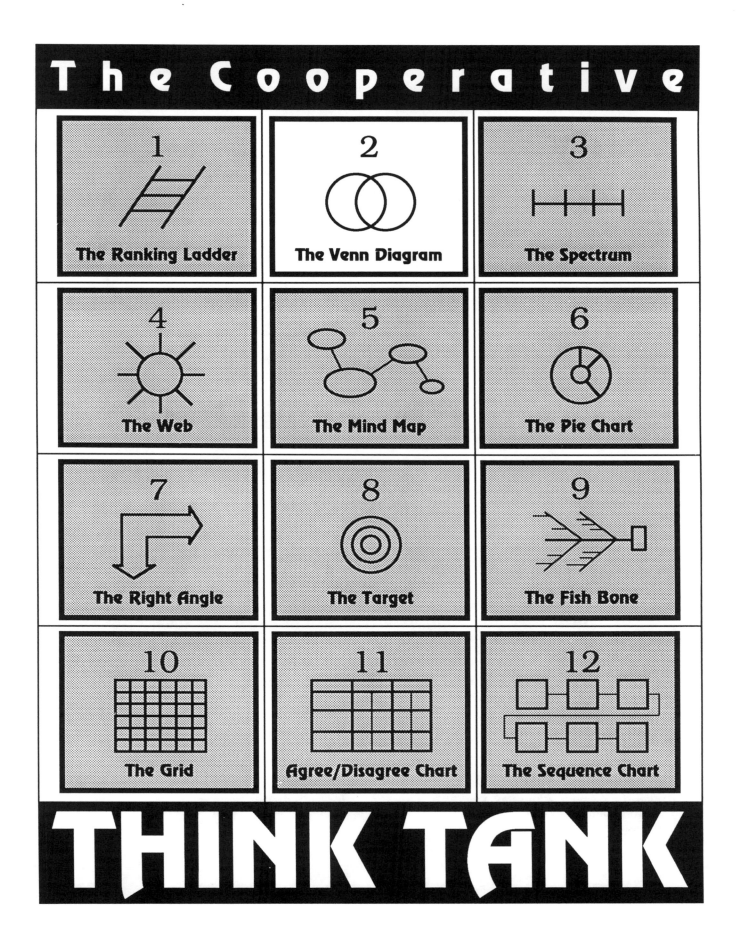

CHAPTER

2

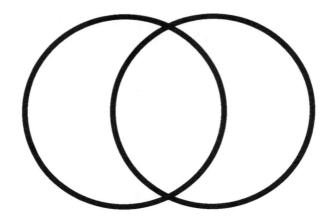

The Venn Diagram

■ **PURPOSE**

To help students visualize likenesses and differences in two or more objects, characters or situations.

■ **VOCABULARY**

Likenesses: Those qualities, attributes, characteristics, values, or special marks that correspond or agree in some respect.

Venn diagram: Two to five interlocked circles of equal size.

■ **THINKING SKILL**

Analysis: Seeing relationships; noticing similarities and differences.

INTRODUCTORY LESSON

Draw an Olympic medallion on the board or overhead or show the students a picture of the Olympic flag. Have them note the five interlocking circles. Explain that this is the Olympic symbol. In relation to visual organizers for thinking it is a "Venn diagram" or five interlocked circles of equal size used to show how objects are alike and different. Explain that the purpose of this lesson is to teach them how to use the Venn diagram to analyze objects and ideas.

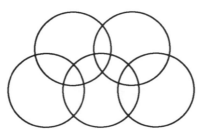

Draw a two-circle Venn diagram on the board or overhead. Place two objects with common traits for all to see. For instance, you could draw a football and baseball or for very young children, a large block and a small block. Label one object X and the other object Y. Label one circle X and one circle Y.

X = football   **Y** = baseball

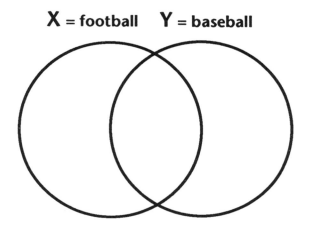

AN ELEMENTARY SCHOOL SAMPLE

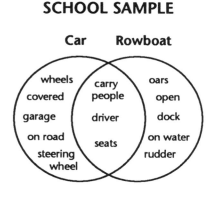

Ask students to identify any trait or characteristic they see as similar or the same in both objects. List those characteristics in the overlapping section of the circles.

Ask students to identify unique traits found only in object X or only in object Y. List these traits in the corresponding circles, but not in the overlapping section.

X = football   **Y** = baseball

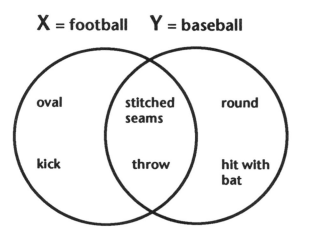

A MIDDLE SCHOOL SAMPLE

Work until all traits are in one of the three areas of the Venn diagram. Label the area unique to circle X "different;" label the area unique to circle Y different and label the central area same or alike.

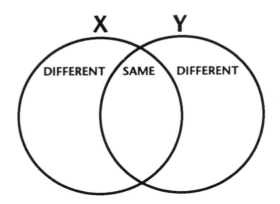

A SECONDARY SCHOOL SAMPLE

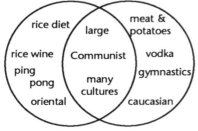

Ask several students to explain in their words how to set up a basic Venn diagram. Ask them to tell where they might use the Venn diagram and how it can help them analyze.

Assign the students to pairs. Use the checker/recorder, worrier and encourager roles. Give the pairs a more abstract task in which they must set up a Venn diagram, (a story with a description of two scenes, two historic characters, two art objects, two word problems, two plants, African and Asian elephants).

1. Hand out a copy of a Venn diagram to each pair of students.

2. Check that they know the steps for using a Venn diagram.

3. Hand out the objects or printed material they will use.

4. Tell them to assign the objects in the correct areas of the circles.

5. Have them list likenesses and differences in the correct areas of the diagram.

6. After most are done, ask two to three pairs to share their results. Discuss any differences.

7. Conduct additional practices as needed with your course content. You have the option to switch student pairs or use a variety of objects.

YOUR IDEA FOR A VENN DIAGRAM

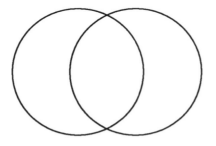

Review or ask students to review the key thinking steps used in preparing a Venn diagram. After you have listed the ideas, identify any required sequences.

1. Prepare your Venn diagram.

2. Label objects A and B; label areas A and B on each circle.

3. List all similarities or likenesses in the center; list differences of each in A and B (or vice versa). It is not important that everyone use the same sequence in filling the sections.

REVIEW & TRANSFER

Pick different topics, objects or situations in different content areas that the students are studying. For instance, primary students could use Venn diagrams with their bird studies to compare types of penguins; in health education, middle schoolers could use Venn diagrams to compare diets; secondary students could use Venn diagrams for literary character study. Practice enough times in class until students are ready for homework assignments using the Venn diagram.

TEST

To test students' mastery of the Venn diagram:

☐ define the key vocabulary words they learned in this lesson.

☐ give a concrete comparison for students to diagram.

☐ give an abstract comparison for students to diagram.

☐ ask students to select two objects or ideas to diagram.

☐ ask students to explain when a Venn diagram is a good thinking tool.

OPTIONAL

For more advanced practice use three, four or five circles for more complex issues. For instance, Advanced Placement Social Studies students could identify the differences and similarities in five world cultures; gifted seventh graders could use the Venn diagram to identify similarities and differences in four characters in a novel. Don't advance to more circles until students have mastered the fewer numbers of circles, however.

APPROPRIATE USE

■ To compare objects, characters, ideas, etc.

■ To contrast objects, characters, ideas, etc.

■ To organize, sort and classify ideas by critical attributes.

NAME _____   CLASS _____

VENN DIAGRAM

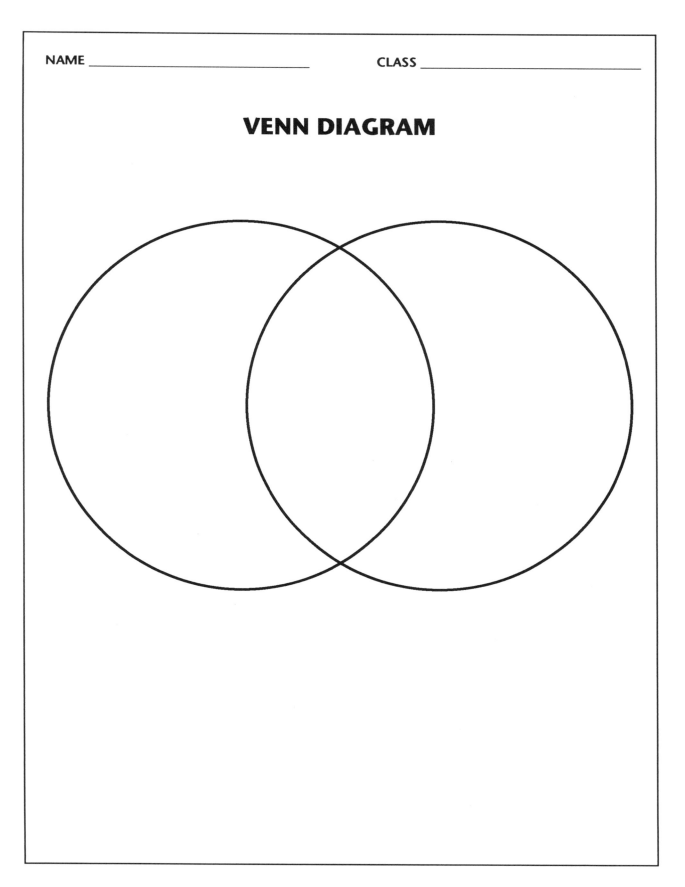

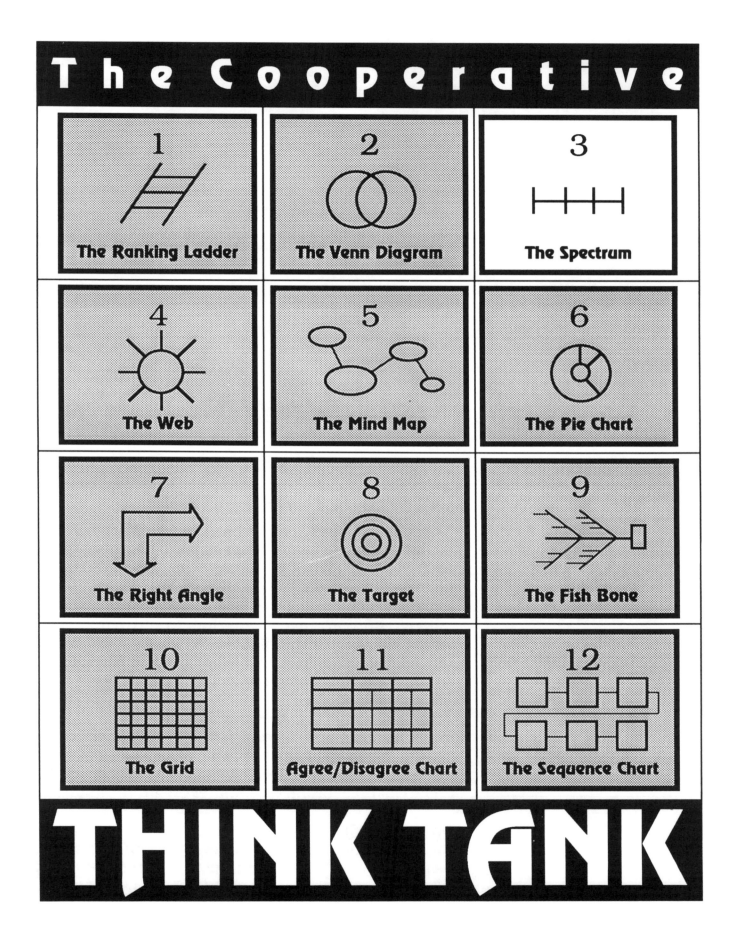

C H A P T E R

3

The Spectrum

■ PURPOSE
To help students see a sequence of events.

■ VOCABULARY

Sequence: one event follows or comes after the other; an order of events.

Milestone: marks indicating events in an order.

Spectrum: a range of varied but related ideas or objects that form a continuous series.

■ THINKING SKILL
Sequencing: Ordering events.

INTRODUCTORY LESSON

Select seven students and line them up, one behind the other in the front of the classroom. Randomly give each student a 3" x 5" index card with a different historic date (1066, 1492, 1776, 1939, 1960, 1984, current year). Tell them to look at their cards without talking and rearrange themselves in order from the lowest number to the highest. When they are rearranged, each should read the date on their card aloud so the class can check if each followed the order.

Tell the students that they are going to learn sequencing or putting objects and dates in an order. Give several examples of times they have used the sequencing skill (alphabet count, checkbook). Ask for additional examples (library, computer program, parades).

On the board or overhead, draw a time line. (For younger students, a clothesline and clothespins are more dramatic!) Mark off equal portions and label each with number sequence "start 1/4, 1/2, 3/4, finish."

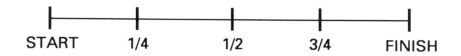

START   1/4   1/2   3/4   FINISH

Ask students to tell a story or describe an event which might use this order of events (i.e., a race).

Define sequencing as a thinking process. Label the steps that go into sequencing an event. Use the race spectrum.

1. Identify the pieces of the whole event.
2. Select important milestones and put them in chronological order.
3. Make visible separations on the spectrum.
4. Label each milestone.

Ask students to picture a spectrum of their lives from birth to today. What milestones could they use? Are they the same distance? What is their sequence?

Tell students they are going to make a spectrum for this school year.

Assign students to random groups of three. Assign the checker/recorder, worrier and encourager.

1. Hand out a spectrum ditto to each pair.
2. Check for understanding of the steps for the sequencing process.
3. Brainstorm one of the following and list the random responses on the board or overhead: chapter titles in your text, holidays, major topics covered in the course, seasons of the year, days of the week.
4. Have each pair construct a spectrum with labeled milestones. When all are finished, have groups exchange and check the results. Each

AN ELEMENTARY SCHOOL SAMPLE

A KID'S DAY

spelling   reading   art   go home
group

A MIDDLE SCHOOL SAMPLE

PROBLEM-SOLVING STEPS

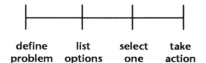

define   list   select   take
problem   options   one   action

group should explain its sequence. If there are difficulties, resolve them with a positive class discussion.

A SECONDARY SCHOOL SAMPLE

MARKETING

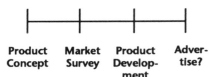

Product Concept   Market Survey   Product Develop- ment   Adver- tise?

REVIEW & TRANSFER

Use one student example to review the thinking process for sequencing. Distribute an additional ditto sheet with more difficult assignments from a textbook chapter, a short story, a scrambled word problem, or a news event. In pairs, practice making the spectrum and explaining to others the result.

When all students have shown they can complete a spectrum, assign homework from classroom content or current events.

TEST

To test students' ability to sequence:

- ☐ Ask students to explain the key vocabulary words from this lesson.
- ☐ Ask students to construct a spectrum from the dates you pull from a current unit.
- ☐ Ask students to sequence events from a story.

YOUR IDEA FOR A SPECTRUM

OPTIONAL

For more advanced practice, assign a daily log of their thinking about ideas learned in your course. Sequence the development of several ideas on parallel charts.

APPROPRIATE USE

- ■ To outline a continuous series or milestones of events.
- ■ To sequence or unscramble events, processes, etc. so they can be easily analyzed, compared or processed.

NAME _____   CLASS _____

THE SPECTRUM

|———|

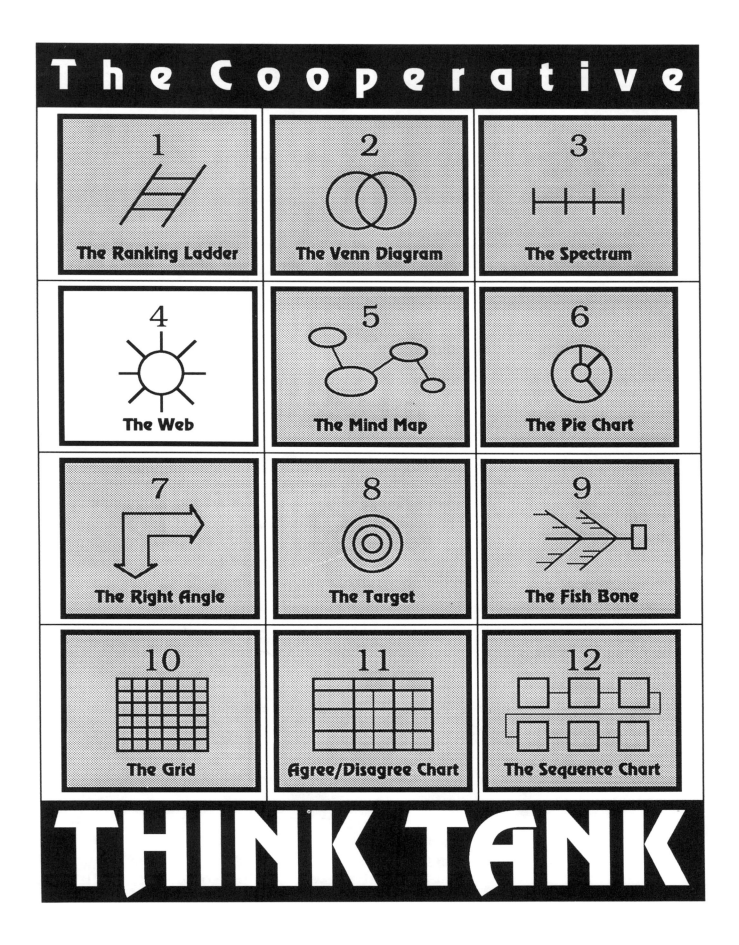

C H A P T E R

4

The Web

■ **PURPOSE**

To help students clarify concepts.

■ **VOCABULARY**

Clarify: to clear up; to understand the specifics.

■ **THINKING SKILLS**

Clarifying concepts, Brainstorming: Generating many ideas without judgment; composing; connecting ideas that appear unrelated to make a coherent story line.

INTRODUCTORY LESSON

On the overhead, show a sample web. Tell the students that they are going to defuzz an idea with the web. Ask them what the word defuzz suggests. (i.e., clear out the fuzz, clean up, etc.)

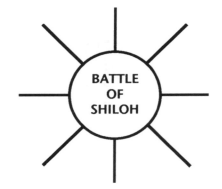

In the center of the wheel, enter the word you want the class to defuzz. Select a noun from a topic they have recently studied. For instance, if you have just completed a unit on the Civil War, select the name of a famous battle. If you have just completed a math unit on whole numbers, put "whole numbers" in the center. In language arts, take the name of a character or place prominent in a story read the previous week.

Review the DOVE Guidelines.

D = DEFER JUDGMENT! Do not use put downs or make positive or negative judgments about others' ideas.

O = OPT FOR OFF-BEAT! As a thinker, be different. Try different ways, seek a new combination.

V = VAST NUMBER'S ARE NEEDED! Go for quantity. From quantity comes quality.

E = EXPAND! Piggyback or hitchhike on others' ideas.

Instruct the class to think of all the words they can which describes the object as they recall it from the previous lesson. Prime the pump with several examples and then allow wait time for thinking by all. Encourage students to write down their first ideas before you call on anyone.

Record the words they supply on to the web. Distribute the chances to respond among many students. If students are too slow in responding, encourage pairs to come up with ideas. Ask each pair to respond in turn.

AN ELEMENTARY SCHOOL SAMPLE

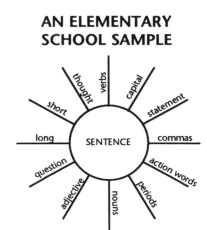

Check to see that all understand how a web works. Clarify as needed by asking students to explain with other examples.

Divide the class into groups of three. Give a sheet of newsprint, marker and tape to each trio. Identify in the group SNAP! (the recorder), CRACKLE! (the worrier), and POP! (the checker). The checker will (a) see that everyone understands the instructions before beginning the task, and (b) all can explain the results. The worrier will keep the focus and see that all three give ideas.

Use the web to **preview** class material, by selecting common noun(s) familiar to the students and related to the next unit of study. For instance, in a health unit, you may want to introduce alcohol. Ask all the teams to defuzz that word. Or you might give each team a different word. For instance, in a unit on nutrition, you might use vegetables, fruits, nuts, meats, etc.

Each group will have five minutes to defuzz the word on newsprint. At the end of three minutes, ask the recorders to post their team webs. Select several team worriers to report on their topics and the checkers to report what the groups did well in completing the task.

Distribute a copy of the web to each trio. Using the title of a story or textbook chapter just completed, demonstrate how they can use the wheel as a **review** tool. Put the title in the center and arrange key words, concepts, or vocabulary around the web. Share the results with the class and process the teamwork in the groups.

A MIDDLE SCHOOL SAMPLE

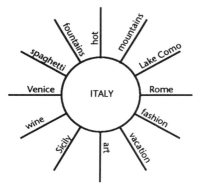

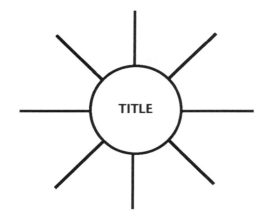

REVIEW & TRANSFER

Assign a new story or chapter title on the web. Assign new groups.

Brainstorm study situations in which students might use the web. In pairs, students should select one situation, develop instructions for the task and prepare a model/sample on newsprint to show the class.

Assign individual homework tasks with the web.

TEST

For testing students' mastery of the web:

☐ Ask students to explain how a web works.

☐ Ask students to construct a web and use a familiar word to defuzz.

☐ Ask students to explain how or when they might use the web in a non-school task.

OPTIONAL

For more advanced practice, assign independent readings from current magazines or essays on topics that the class is studying. Instruct students to construct a web on the key or main idea.

For special uses, use the web to introduce a new unit. The whole class may web its prior knowledge on the topic. Use the web to review a unit. Give each trio a specific subtopic to web and review before the entire class.

APPROPRIATE USE

■ To generate multiple ideas.

■ To preview unit by listing attributes of appropriate topics.

■ To review material by listing attributes of assigned topics.

A SECONDARY SCHOOL SAMPLE

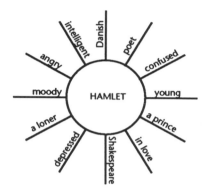

YOUR IDEA FOR A WEB

NAME _____   CLASS _____

THE WEB

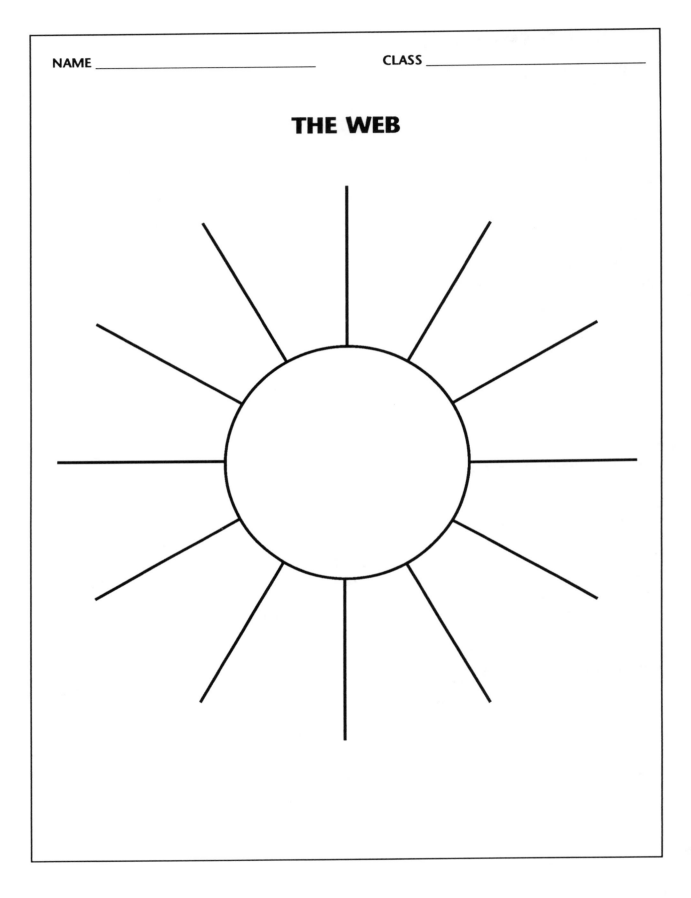

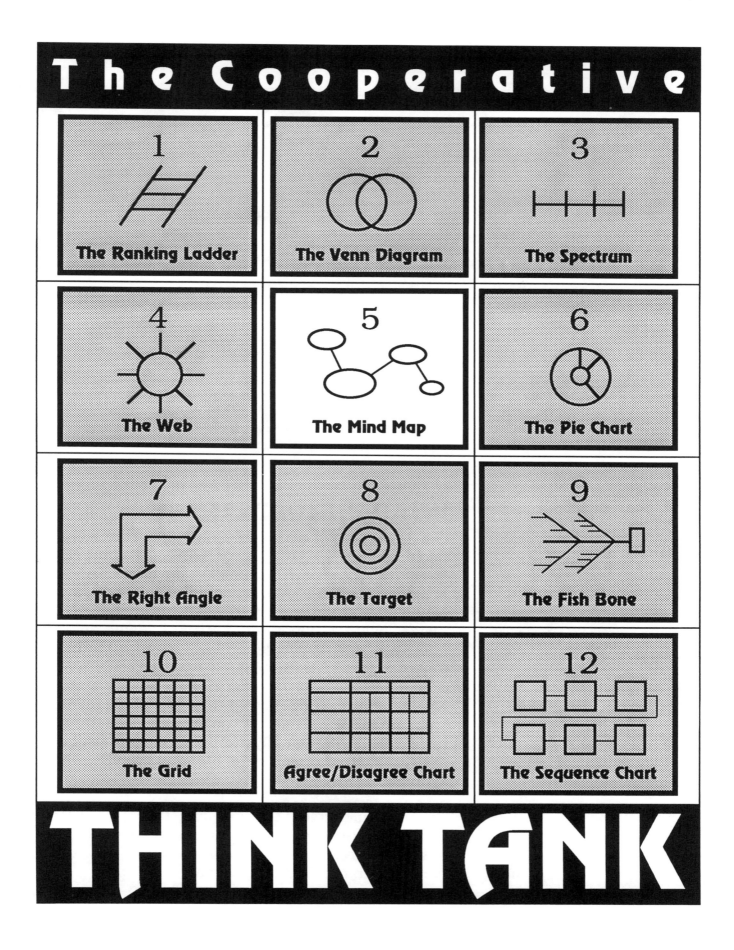

C H A P T E R

5

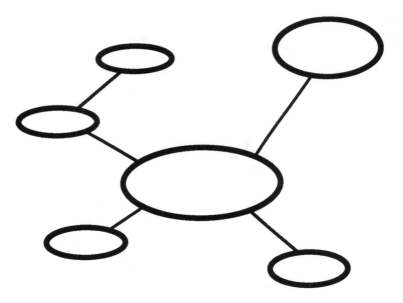

The Mind Map

<table>
<tr>
<td>

■ **PURPOSE**

To help students clarify relationships between concepts.

■ **VOCABULARY**

Relationship: **the way in which objects or concepts are connected.**

■ **THINKING SKILL**

Seeing relationships

</td>
</tr>
</table>

INTRODUCTORY LESSON

On the overhead or board, show this statement "A house is like _____." Pick a second object familiar to the students and fill in the blank. "A house is like an airplane." Ask students to give you ways in which this statement is true (i.e., both have seats inside" (factual, concrete); "both are people holders" (more abstract, application); "both represent humans' ability to create" (symbolic).

Explain to the students that they are seeing relationships or the ways that two objects or ideas are connected. There are usually multiple connections. Some are very factual or concrete; others more abstract or symbolic.

Tell the students that they are going take the web from the previous lesson one step further and use it as a tool to help see relationships among ideas. The new, expanded web is called a mind map.

Display a completed mind map. Point out the major features. (A) key idea, (B) sub ideas, (C) connecting details, and (D) use of connectors. For instance:

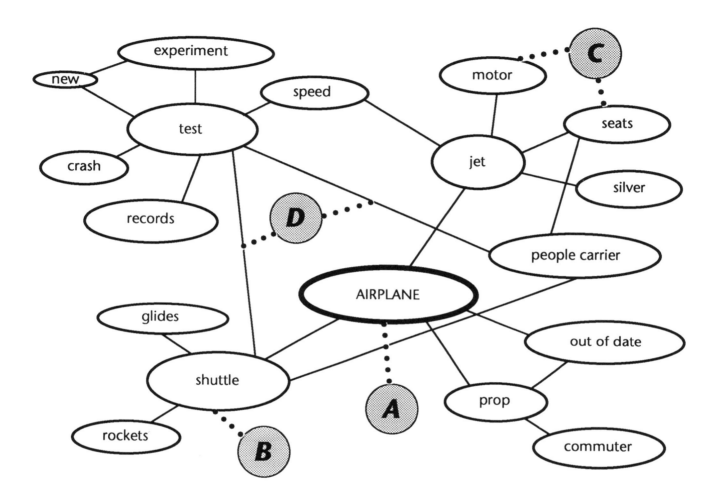

Let them know that this is a challenging task, but you believe they can do well. Explain the purpose: the map is a thinking tool that helps connect ideas and see relationships. They might use the tool for note taking in a lecture or from a reading assignment, to explore new ideas, or to plan a course of action. Many writers use this technique as a pre-writing task to generate and organize ideas.

Start the map skill with an emphasis on prior knowledge. On the board or overhead, sketch the first piece of a map.

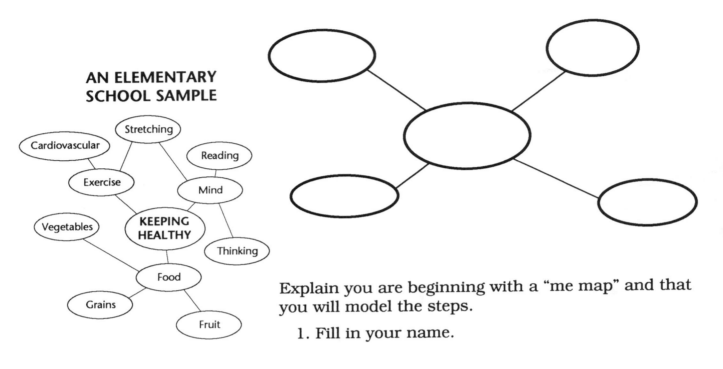

AN ELEMENTARY SCHOOL SAMPLE

Explain you are beginning with a "me map" and that you will model the steps.

1. Fill in your name.

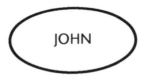

2. Fill in the key topics.

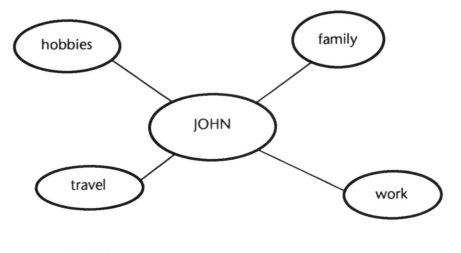

LIBRARY
BRYAN COLLEGE
DAYTON, TENN. 3732

3. Ask the students to ask you a question about any area. You can pass or put your answer on the map. For instance: What's your favorite hobby? (jogging) What are your children's names? (Toby, Yvonne). Keep responding until your demo map is filled. Use a second color to connect related answers.

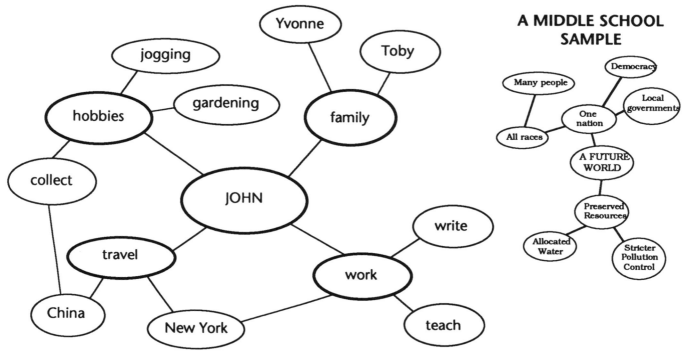

A MIDDLE SCHOOL SAMPLE

4. Distribute newsprint sheets and two markers to each trio. Have each group invent a name for itself and enter the individual names in the next set.

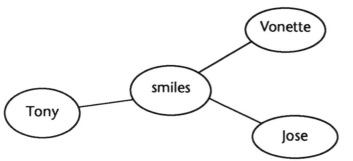

5. In round-robin fashion, the group members should interview each other. Whenever they find a similarity or likeness, use the second color marker to connect the likenesses. Allow 10 minutes.

A SECONDARY SCHOOL SAMPLE

6. After 10 minutes, have the groups list in a corner of the newsprint how they worked well together and sign their names. Post the newsprint sheets and ask one or two groups to highlight the likenesses it found in the group.

Discuss any difficulties the groups experienced. Resolve the difficulties as a class or give time to think the problems over at home.

Divide the class into new pairs. Give each pair a copy of a mind map. Instruct each pair to select a topic they know a lot about (i.e., the school, a favorite rock group, the city, town or neighborhood). Construct maps with no set subgroups.

Match pairs into fours. Allow each pair five minutes to share its map, explain its thinking about how words are connected or related.

Assign each four a story or a text chapter to read. Give the fours a large sheet of blank newsprint and instruct them to map out the material. Assign worrier, checker, recorder and timekeeper roles. After 20 minutes, post completed sheets and select reporters to explain *what* the connections are and *why* they made them. Encourage clarifying questions from the class.

Discuss other uses of the mind map with the class.

REVIEW & TRANSFER

Have student pairs make mind maps from (a) a major news story; (b) a team homework assignment; or (c) a lecture or film or to review a unit.

After all students show skill in using the map, make an individual homework assignment. Have each student pick a common household item and construct a map to share in class.

TEST

To test students' mastery of the mind map:

☐ Ask students to explain key vocabulary words from this lesson.

☐ Ask students to list the four key steps for constructing a mind map.

☐ Give the students a familiar object to map. Have them indicate with letters how they used each step in the process.

☐ For older students, ask them to distinguish how one describes a concrete object vs. an abstract object.

YOUR IDEA FOR A MIND MAP

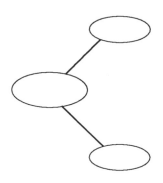

OPTIONAL

For advanced practice, play tapes or records of poems by American writers. As students listen, they should construct mind maps. Assign students to conduct an interview of important career people in your area.

APPROPRIATE USE

■ To generate ideas that are related.

■ To show relationships among ideas.

■ To review prior knowledge or a completed unit.

■ To gather information in a random, but organizing manner, similar to structured overview.

NAME _____ CLASS _____

THE MIND MAP

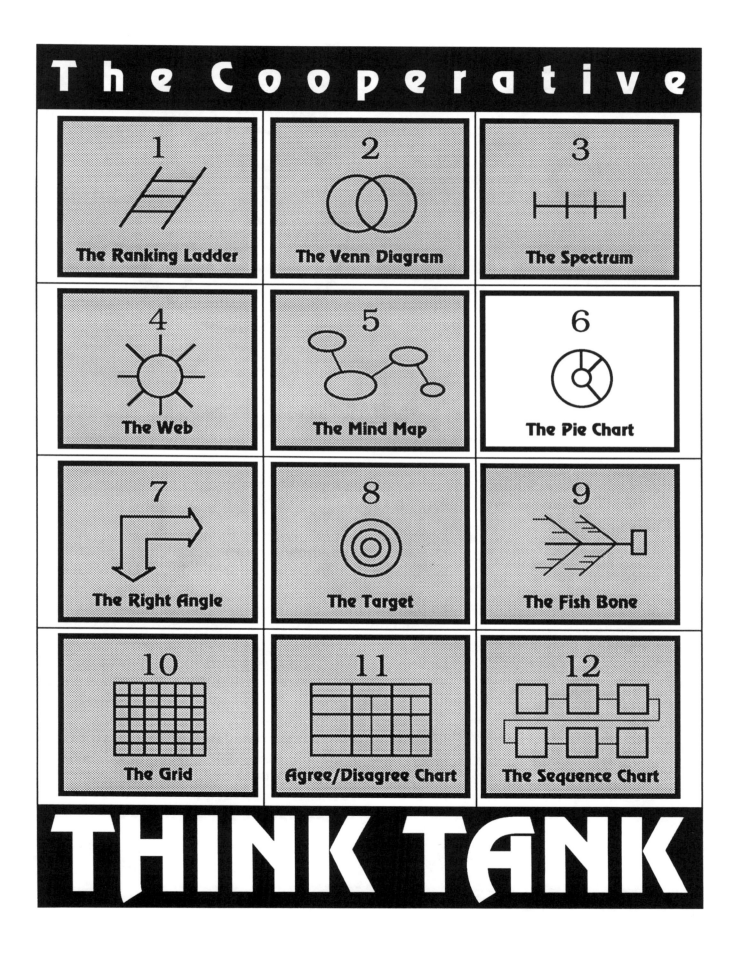

CHAPTER

6

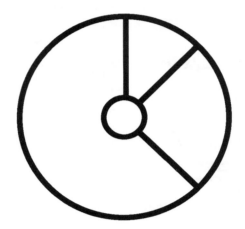

The Pie Chart

■ **PURPOSE**

To help students estimate the relationship of parts to the whole.

■ **VOCABULARY**

Analysis: to break an idea or object into its parts; to see how parts relate to the whole.

■ **THINKING SKILLS**

Seeing relationships, Analyzing

INTRODUCTORY LESSON

Bring a real pie or use a cardboard cutout of a pie. Ask one student to show how to divide the pie into four parts, another into six and a third into eight parts.

Explain on the overhead how a pie chart can help divide concepts as well as objects into related parts.

Define the word *analysis* and explain how in this lesson they will learn to use a pie chart as a concept analysis tool.

Identify a current TV show familiar to the students. Make the selection age appropriate (e.g., Sesame Street for primary students or CBS network news for older students). You may select a short video or film to show (e.g., "The Muppet Movie" or "The Red Balloon").

Review the DOVE Guidelines :

D = DEFER JUDGMENT! Do not use put-downs or make positive or negative judgments about others' ideas.

O = OPT FOR OFF-BEAT! As a thinker, be different. Try different ways, seek a new combination.

V = VAST NUMBER! Go for quantity. From quantity comes quality.

E = EXPAND! Piggyback or hitchhike on others' ideas.

Brainstorm a list of characters from the selected show. Record the list on the board.

Draw a pie chart on the board or overhead. Enter the topic/show in the center circle. Invite students to enter a name from the list of characters onto the pie chart. After entering the name, the student should estimate the importance or the amount of time the character appears on the show. The larger or more important the time span of the character, the bigger the bigger the piece of pie devoted to it.

AN ELEMENTARY SCHOOL SAMPLE

WHAT NUTRITIOUS FOODS DO YOU LIKE?
• water
• potatoes
• watermelon
• chili beans

A MIDDLE SCHOOL SAMPLE

WHAT MAKES A GOOD TEAM?
• Active listening
• Helping each other
• Encouraging gestures
• Supporting words

Discuss how this division of the pie chart is alike or different from dividing the pie into equal parts.

**A SECONDARY
SCHOOL SAMPLE**

**WHAT IS IMPORTANT
TO ME IN MY FUTURE?**
• Going to a vocational
  school or college
• Making lots of
  money
• Helping others
• Enjoying my career
• Having a family

Divide the class into threes or fours. Give each group a copy of the pie chart and a ruler. Assign the worrier, checker, recorder and materials gopher roles.

Each group will select one character from the "master" pie. First, they will brainstorm words to describe the character. Second, they will enter the words on the pie and agree on how important the characteristic is by dividing the pie into sections.

Match groups in pairs to share their pies and explain what reasons they had for (a) selecting the descriptive words, and (b) make the slices different sizes.

REVIEW & TRANSFER

Select a textbook reading about a historic figure or literary character from a biography or a short story. Give each new pair a ditto copy. Instruct them to select a character and the descriptions and mark off the pie slices. Older students can write short explanations for the selection.

After all students show a mastery of this skill, assign textbook homework that requires each to use the pie.

Discuss when students can best use this pie strategy (percentage, proportional analysis).

TEST

To test students' mastery of this lesson:

☐ Ask students to explain key vocabulary words from this lesson.

☐ Ask students to explain how the pie chart aids thinking.

☐ Ask the students to give two examples that demonstrate the pie as a thinking tool.

☐ Ask students to complete a pie chart on a test situation you create.

OPTIONAL

For advanced practice, assign independent readings that will allow students to use their pie charting skills.

APPROPRIATE USE

 **YOUR IDEA FOR A PIE CHART**

- ■ To show proportionate relationships.
- ■ To analyze the importance of component parts in a story, process, problem, etc.

NAME _____   CLASS _____

THE PIE CHART

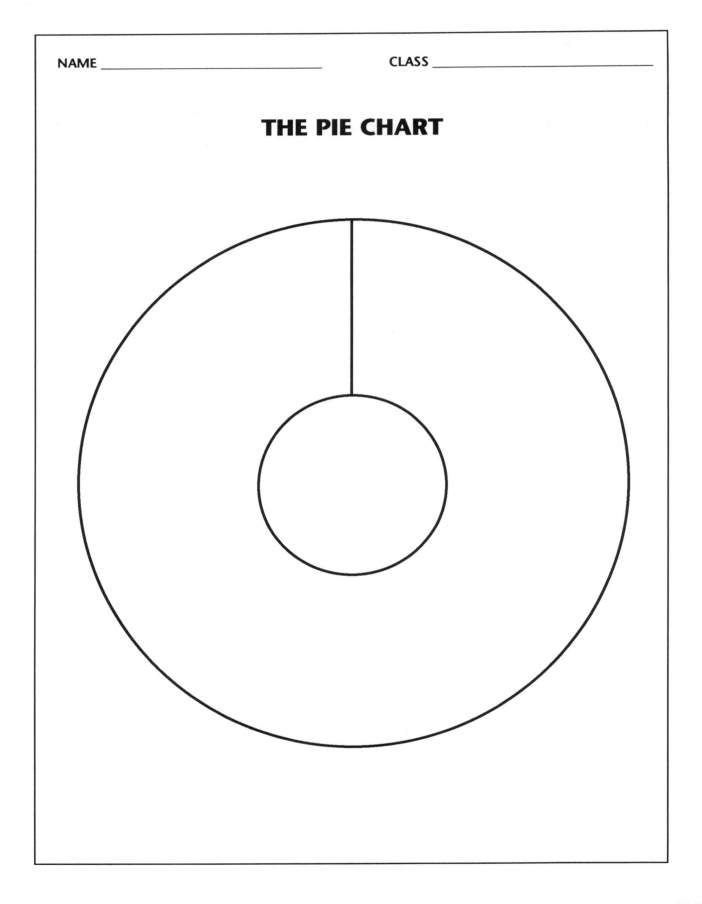

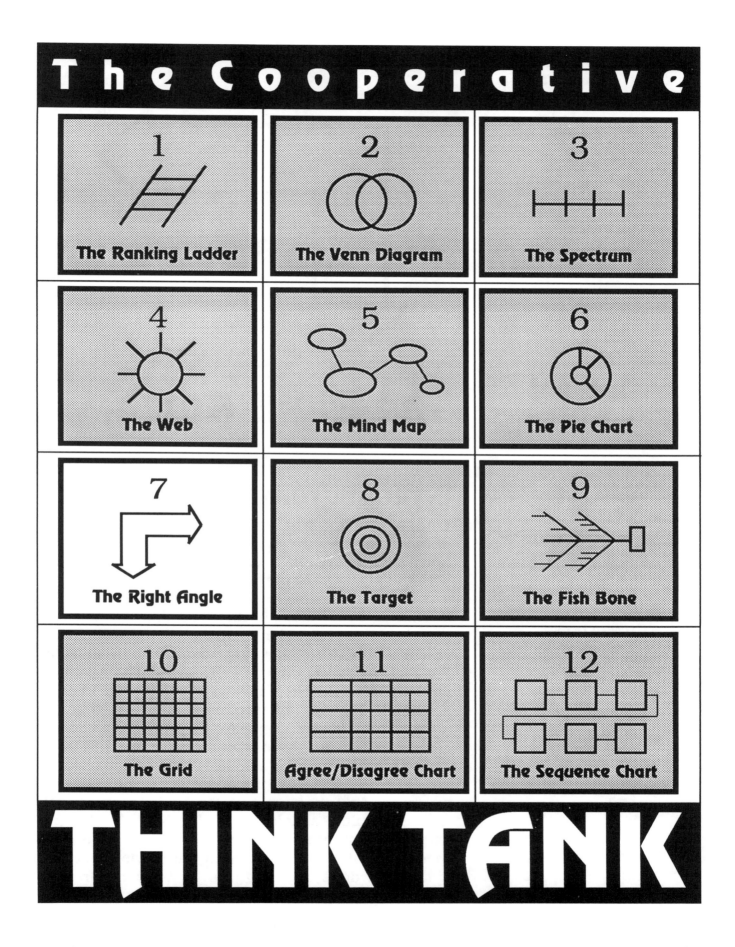

C H A P T E R

7

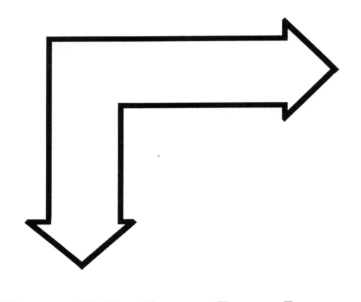

The Right Angle

■ PURPOSE
To help students explore the implications of ideas and make personal applications to those ideas.

■ VOCABULARY

Implications: To have a resulting effect on; to imply; to twist or fold together; intertwine; entangle.

Applications: The act of putting something to use.

■ THINKING SKILL

Exploring implications; making transfer

INTRODUCTORY LESSON

Line six students into two right-angled groups in front of the class. Give the student at the outer end of one line a sign that reads "Leonardo da Vinci." Give a sign with the words "the submarine" to the second student in that line and a sign with "sharp observer" to the third. Tell the students in the class about da Vinci as an artist, scientist and inventor or ask the students to read a short excerpt on da Vinci from an encyclopedia. For each of the accomplishments, give each remaining student a card that explains some of his special accomplishments: Philosopher–kept a log, thought about the challenges of space, and proposed a new set of ethics. Ask the class to brainstorm three qualities of a good thinker that da Vinci must have had in order to do all that he did. List the answers on the board or overhead. Ask students to select which three of the answers could best help them in life. Make three signs with the choices and invite three students to hold these in front of the class. Point out to the class that it has just done some right-angle thinking. In this thinking, they transferred information about da Vinci to the applications in their own lives.

On the board or overhead, show the right-angle graphic. Next, ask someone to identify a popular TV show. Write the title in the upper section (A). Have the class identify key ideas about the show's characters, story line, importance, etc. Put this next to the main topic (B). Next, ask the students to expand on one of those ideas with details from their research or previous experiences (C). Finally, have students apply the detailed concept to their own lives (D).

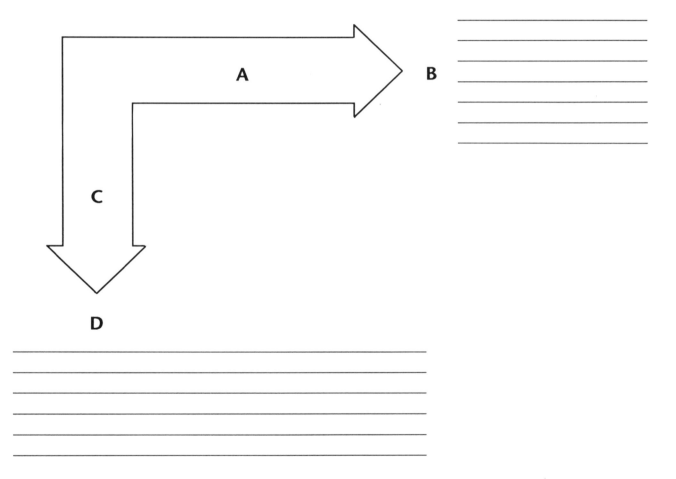

Check for understanding of the process before you break the class into groups of three and assign the recorder, encourager and checker/worrier roles. Review your guidelines for cooperation and distribute newsprint, markers and tape to each group.

Distribute the name of a person important to one of the content areas (math, art, science, history, literature, sports, etc.) to each group. Assign the group to gather information about this person (you may want to assign encyclopedia articles). Each group will agree on the three most important characteristics or accomplishments of its person and write these in the A and B positions.

AN ELEMENTARY SCHOOL SAMPLE

Walter Payton ran his super hill every day.

Reading about star atheletes who are good role models

Walter Payton and Michael Jordan practice extra hard each day. Both hate drugs.

I could take more responsibility for staying in shape

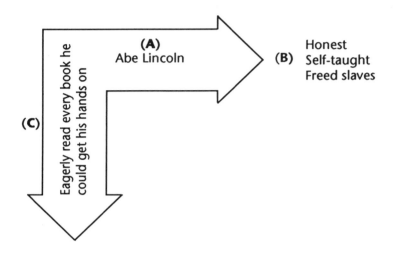

(C)

Eagerly read every book he could get his hands on

(A) Abe Lincoln

(B) Honest
Self-taught
Freed slaves

(D) I could expand my reading by thinking of how eager Abe Lincoln would have been at having the opportunity of reading all the books available to me

On the other side of the angle, they will expand on one of those ideas (from B) with details from their research. Finally, they will brainstorm the applications of the right-angle thinking to their own lives in section D.

After each group has agreed on its answers, the checker should ensure that each member can explain the choices. Select groups to share completed right angles with the entire class. Encourage positive feedback and discussion. Collect and evaluate all the graphics while students evaluate the quality of their contributions within the group.

A MIDDLE SCHOOL SAMPLE

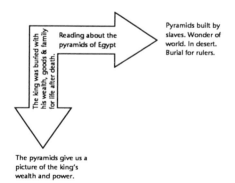

The king was buried with his wealth, goods & family for life after death.

Reading about the pyramids of Egypt

Pyramids built by slaves. Wonder of world. In desert. Burial for rulers.

The pyramids give us a picture of the king's wealth and power.

REVIEW & TRANSFER

Select readings from your texts, news articles or other media (e.g., a short story, a magazine article, a novel or biography). Pick a theme or character for the students to focus on or allow them to pick their own.

In the first angle, they will identify the focus person, place or concept. Next to it they will list key ideas about the topic. In the second angle, they will detail the importance of one of the key topics in the context of the entire work. Finally, in the bottom space, they will explain the relationship/importance of the elaborated idea to their own lives. Display the graphics and select several groups to explain their products. Conclude each transfer assignment with a discussion of the benefits of using this graphic and/or when they could best use the graphic outside of your classroom.

TEST

To test the students' individual knowledge and skill with the right angle:

- ☐ Ask the students to define the terms *right angle*, *transfer* and *implications* (do this with a complete the sentence, fill in the blank or true/false).

- ☐ Ask the students to explain how the right angle helps their thinking.

- ☐ Ask the students to complete a right angle with the following information about Abe Lincoln: lawyer; president and author; wrote the Emancipation Proclamation and the Gettysburg Address; made many enemies; freed the slaves. The students must fill in the application section (D).

- ☐ Ask the students to create a right angle that gives instructions for its completion.

OPTIONAL

For advanced practice, assign independent readings of biographies that will allow students to use this graphic organizer. Assign the students to interview a parent or community leader and use the right angle to organize their thinking.

APPROPRIATE USE

- ■ To analyze characters (real or fictional) who model transferable values beneficial to students.

- ■ To analyze ideas or beliefs that allow exploration of implications and the transfer of values.

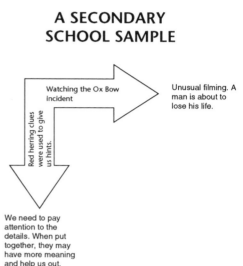

A SECONDARY SCHOOL SAMPLE

Watching the Ox Bow incident

Unusual filming. A man is about to lose his life.

Red herring clues were used to give us hints.

We need to pay attention to the details. When put together, they may have more meaning and help us out.

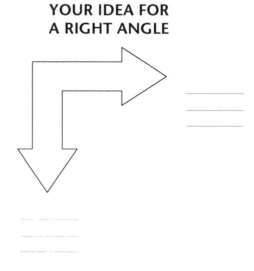

YOUR IDEA FOR A RIGHT ANGLE

NAME _____   CLASS _____

THE RIGHT ANGLE

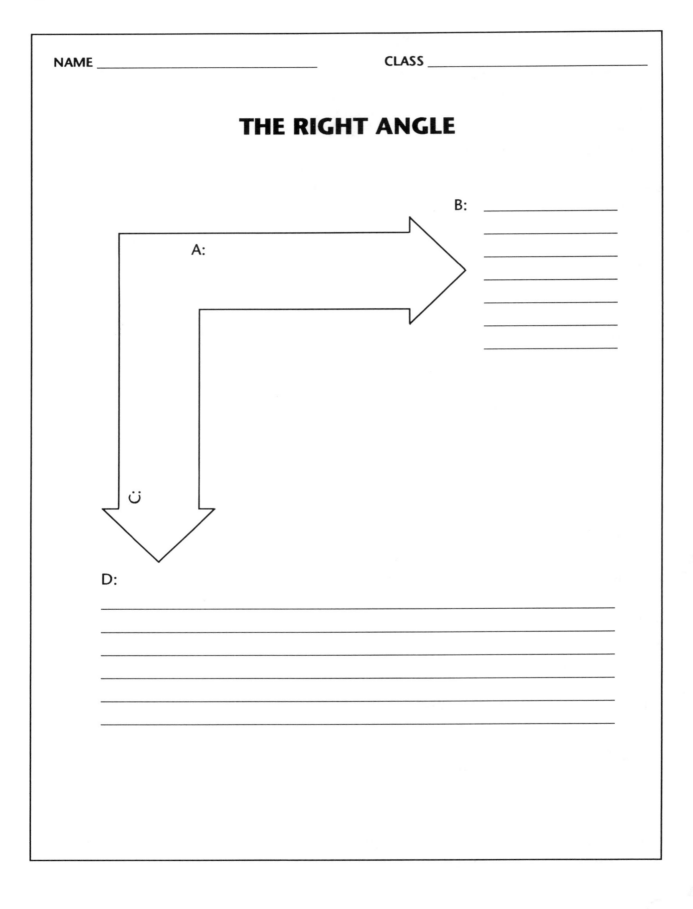

B: _____

A:

C:

D:

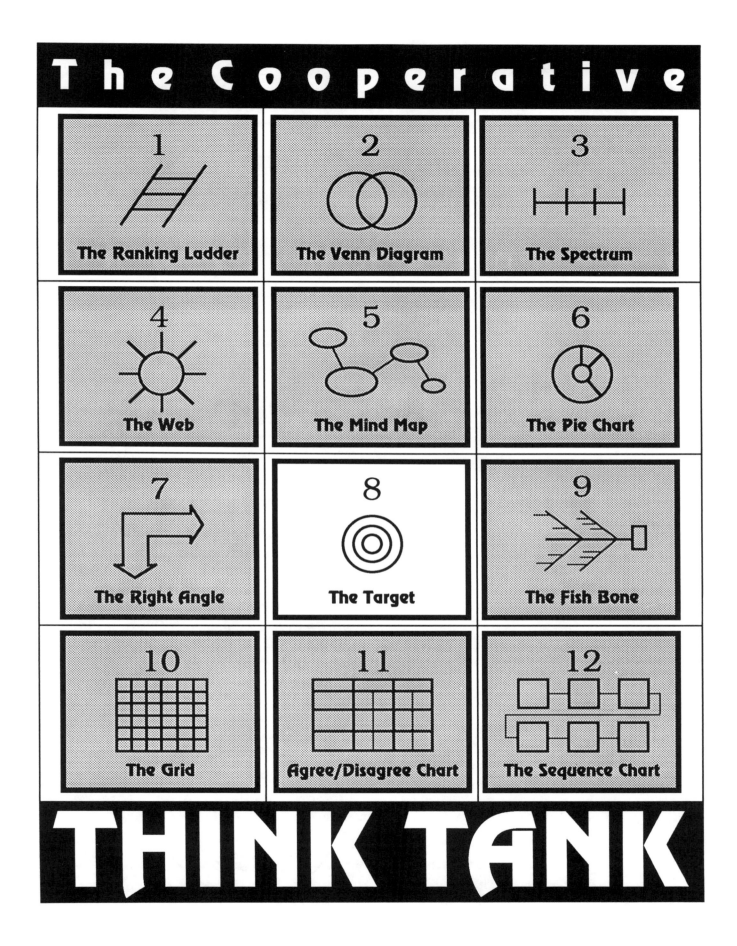

C H A P T E R

8

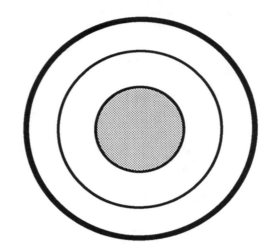

The Target

■ **PURPOSE**

To weigh important facts, ideas or beliefs.

■ **VOCABULARY**

Target: An objective, goal

Evaluate: To make a judgment, to weigh the worth or importance of an object or idea.

■ **THINKING SKILL**

Evaluating: Judging the value or importance; explaining why a choice was made

INTRODUCTORY LESSON

Draw a target on the board or display the sample on an overhead. Ask students to describe uses for a target (i.e., to shoot at, a goal to reach). Give the students three words (i.e., three characters from a story, three events from history, three emotions) and ask several to (a) place the words in the target with the most important word in the center of the target and the least important in the outer circle; and (b) explain the reasons for the placements.

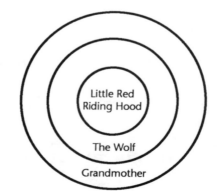

Explain to the students that the target is a graphic thinking tool which helps them clarify the importance or value of ideas. In more complex targets with five or more words, the target will help them group words of similar importance.

Assign students of mixed abilities to pairs. Assign a checker/recorder and a worrier/encourager. Give each recorder a copy of the target. Check that all teams know the procedures. Remind them that both members must agree and be able to explain their placement of words. For checking, ask, "What is most important for our team?" Elicit answers to the question. Place the most important example in the inner circle and work outwards to the least important. In school what is most important—getting good grades, having lots of friends, or obeying the school rules?

Review the responses by asking several recorders to explain their teams' target answers.

Give each team a second target. Use rank orders from current events or from one of your current topics in class, i.e., read a story and target the characters most important to the story, the least important, the middle ones. Only the middle group (the middle circle in the target) may have more than one character. List five steps used for solving a math problem. Target the most important, the least important, etc. Be sure that both partners agree and can explain the placement.

REVIEW & TRANSFER

Invite each group to make a list of the thinking processes/steps used with the target. On the target have each team place the most important step, the least important step, and so on. Do not accept that all the steps are equally important. The idea is to force the choices so that the students will think more deeply about each step. Ask a team to put its response on the board and to defend the arrangement. Ask for different arrangements and/or different reasons. Come to an agreement on the best arrangement.

AN ELEMENTARY SCHOOL SAMPLE

WHAT ARE HELPFUL "SAY NO" SKILLS?

Problem-solving skill
Broken record
Change "friends"
Talk to parent
Stay away

A MIDDLE SCHOOL SAMPLE

WHAT IS IMPORTANT FOR SUCCESS?

Positive friends
Listen to parents
Study hard
Study skills
Stay out of trouble
Be honest

**A SECONDARY
SCHOOL SAMPLE**

**WHO WAS THE BIGGEST
CONTRIBUTOR TO
MACBETH'S TRAGEDY?**

**His wife
McDuff
Greed
Power
The witches
His soldiers**

**YOUR IDEA FOR
A TARGET**

Now, assign students to complete additional targets from the materials in your classroom. Check that they know the vocabulary words and the process for completing a target. As you extend practices you may increase the number of items to be targeted and/or the complexity of the reasons. Instead of one reason for each placement, you might insist on two or three.

After the students have become fluent with the method, structure homework assignments in which the students use the target as the key organizational tool. For example, in a chapter on Egypt, ask them to read about the historic monuments and use the target to identify the most important ones. Each should be prepared to use text material to back up the placement. In a play, you may ask the students to read for themes. Each should pick out at least three themes in the play, place them on the target and prepare a rationale. Very young students can learn to use this organizer with simple, concrete topics; advanced secondary schoolers can use it to evaluate complex issues connecting their subject matter to real-world issues.

TEST

To test individuals' use of the target:

- ☐ Have students define the term *evaluate*.

- ☐ Ask students to explain how the target organizer can help with evaluation.

- ☐ Select five ideas or topics from class work which was not previously targeted. Have students place the items into their targets and explain their reasoning (one reason for each placement).

- ☐ Give students a blank target and five topics to use. Have them write instructions for an absent classmate on how to use the target.

OPTIONAL

For advanced practice, assign teams to create target topics from the class material. Have teams exchange lists and complete the targets. Assign magazine articles on current affairs. Each team will have a different article on a similar topic. They will select five key arguments made by the author and rate them on the target. In class, each team will share its target.

APPROPRIATE USE

- ■ To evaluate the importance of an idea, topic, etc. and be able to explain why it is or is not important. (Be sure that there are sufficient topics, ideas, facts, arguments, etc. in the material to effectively use the target.)

- ■ To build arguments with supporting evidence by grouping appropriate ideas and information together.

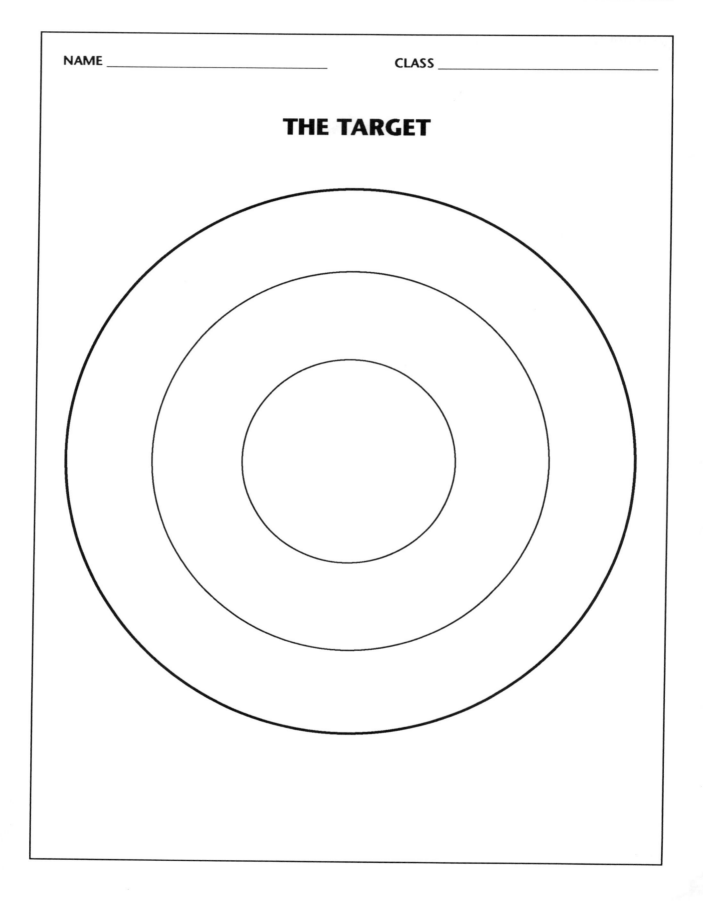

NAME _____   CLASS _____

THE TARGET

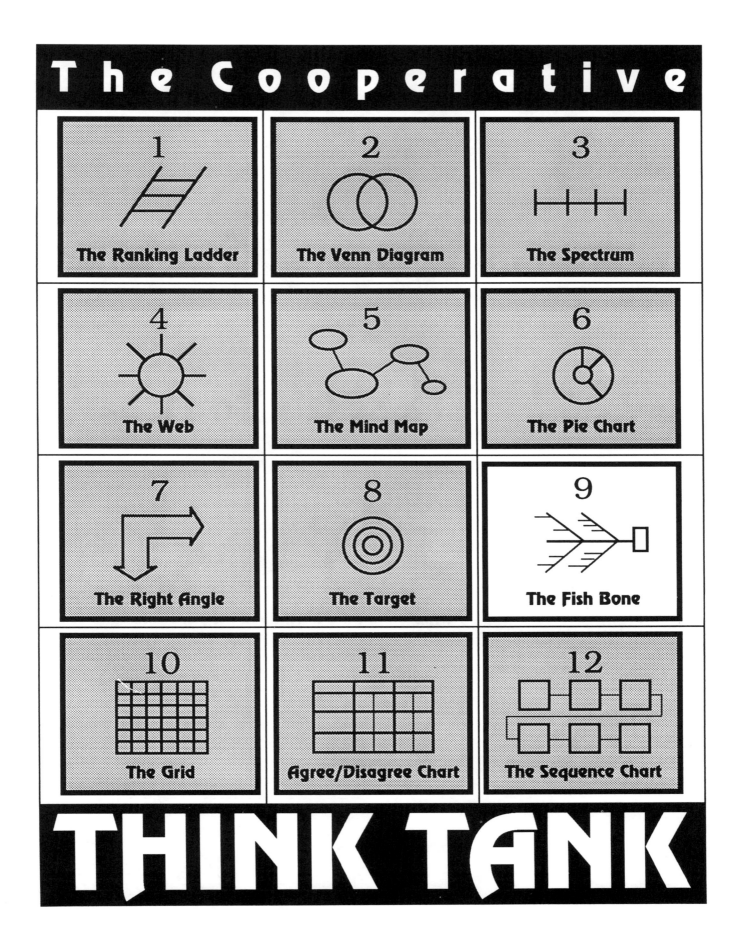

C H A P T E R

9

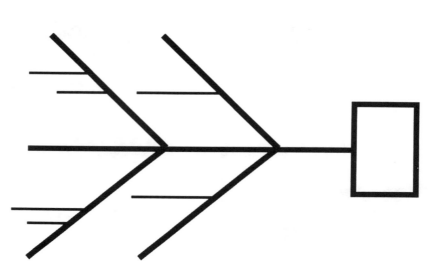

The Fish Bone

■ **PURPOSE**

To help students identify separate causes and effects.

■ **VOCABULARY**

Fish bone: A graphic organizer used to separate possible causes from each other.

Cause: An event, person or object that makes something happen.

■ **THINKING SKILL**

Identifying causes

INTRODUCTORY LESSON

Draw a fish bone on the board or show it on the overhead. Make it very large. Ask the students to speculate why this graphic organizer is called a fish bone. Explain to the class that the fish bone is a common thinking tool used in business, especially when people are working in problem-solving teams to identify possible causes of a problem. Indicate you are going to show them how to use the fish bone chart as a problem-solving tool with many applications in the classroom and in the work world.

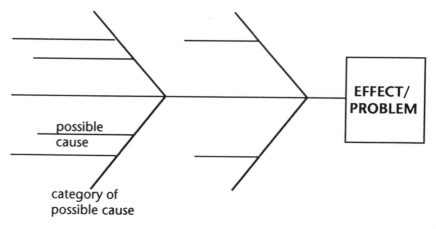

In the head of the fish, labeled effect, write the phrase "car accident." At the end of each major "bone" write one of the category words: people, machines, environment, and others. Indicate that these are words to give clues. Was the accident caused by something the people did? Was there something wrong with the cars (machines)? Was the problem caused by the environment (road, weather, etc.)? Show an overhead of a car accident. Ask for ideas about the possible causes.

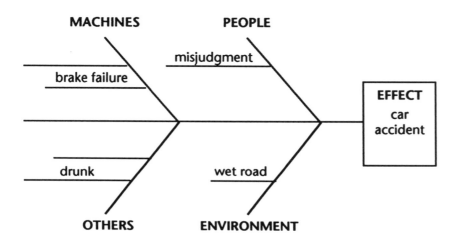

As a student volunteers an answer, ask the student to tell you which category or group to write the answer under. Follow the student's directions and write the answer on one of the smaller bones. Ask other students to repeat the two-step answer and record what they say. Note to the students that you did not disagree with the placement. Latter group discussion will allow time for arguing placement and making changes.

Assign the students to groups of four. Assign and review the roles of checker, recorder, materials gopher, and encourager. Have the students check in their groups for understanding of the responsibilities of each member's role. Invite the gophers to pick up the groups' supplies: newsprint, markers and tape, or photocopies of the fish bone master. Review the DOVE guidelines.

AN ELEMENTARY
SCHOOL SAMPLE

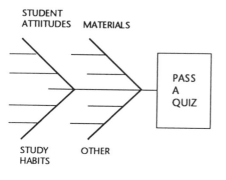

Instruct each group to continue the accident analysis on the fish bone. For the next 10 minutes, the groups, answering in turn, should fill in the small bones with possible causes of the effect.

At the end of the time, instruct the groups to review the listed items and agree on the final placement of each. If agreement is difficult, they may list any item in as many groups as needed.

After the discussion is over, conduct *individual* rankings. Ask each group member to select three items from the total list (they can be from different categories or all from one) which he/she believes are the *most likely causes* of the accident. After selecting the three, each individual should rank them. When all have done their private rankings, each group should make an unduplicated list of only items that were ranked by individuals. Allow 10 minutes for this step.

Carl	Ray	Group List
1. wet road	1. drunk	• wet road
2. drunk	2. brake failure	• drunk
3. fell asleep	3. sun in eyes	• fell asleep
		• break failure
		• sun in eyes

A MIDDLE
SCHOOL SAMPLE

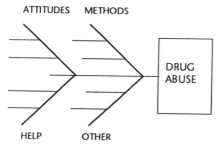

After the unduplicated list is made, allow an additional 10 minutes for the groups to discuss which items from the list are most important. At the end of the time, each person will have a chance to vote on the top three *most likely causes*. No combinations are allowed.

End the discussion after 10 minutes. Each person will select the three causes he/she thought were the most likely causes. A person may vote only three times. To vote, the recorder will read off the first item of the unduplicated list. Any person in the group who is using one of his/her three votes for that item will raise his/her hand. The recorder will add and mark the vote total on the group's list. The group will vote for each item on the list in this way. After all votes are recorded, the recorder will star the top three choices.

In the next 10 minutes, the group will put together its arguments for the agreed upon causes. Every member of the group will be responsible for the explanation. At the end of the time allotted, call each group to the front to explain its choices. When the group is in front of the class, you may select the one or two people who will explain the group's selections. As a group is speaking, the listening students must attend to differences for a rebuttal.

When the presentations are done, open up an all-class discussion about the differences in the conclusions. After 15 minutes, end the discussions and assign the groups to write a summary of the major disagreements.

Conclude the analysis by instructing each group to compliment all members in that group and to staple all of the group's work. Instruct the gophers to place the group work on your desk.

REVIEW & TRANSFER

Ask the students to review the key steps in making a fish bone and *explain* why each is important.

1. Identify the effect.
2. Identify the category names.
3. Use a round-robin to suggest possible causes.
4. Discuss the suggested causes.
5. Privately rank the causes.
6. Use a round-robin to make an unduplicated list of the causes.
7. Vote for a final rank order.
8. Prepare an explanation of the choices

Keep this list of steps visible in the classroom for use during the practice and transfer lessons.

To give your students more practice with the fish bone

A SECONDARY SCHOOL SAMPLE

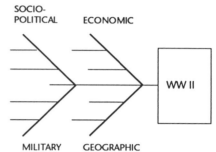

YOUR IDEA FOR A FISHBONE

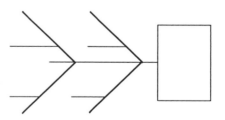

free of content, select common events from their day-to-day experiences, current events or non-technical tasks for practice (e.g., drug overdose, nuclear explosion, overabundance of waste, winning the Super Bowl).

When the students display an ease of use with the fish bone method, take them into language arts, science and social studies. Use the fish bone as a tool to engage the content in a more thoughtful way. (Why did Rome fall? Why did Hamlet die? Why did . . . ?)

As students show more fluency and flexibility with the fish bone, you can expect more metacognitive work from them. Elicit discussions that encourage students to talk about why they made certain decisions, how they organized their thinking and which parts of their thinking were more precise.

TEST

To test students' basic knowledge of the fish bone:

☐ Ask students to define *fish bone, analysis, cause, effect.*

☐ Ask students to explain why a fish bone analysis is an important thinking tool (e.g., it's a visible way to break down causes and effects; it helps separate possible causes).

☐ Ask students to draw a fish bone and to give instructions for completing an analysis of what might have caused a student to earn a straight A report card.

OPTIONAL

If you teach language arts, begin with simple causes and effects (i.e., the three pigs). As you move through the curriculum, select more difficult stories for a cause-effect analysis (i.e., in a senior literature class, you might start with such short stories as Poe's "Murder in Rue Morgue" and progress to *Death of a Salesman* and *Hamlet.* In the first, the cause of the murders; in *Death of a Salesman,* the cause of Willy's failure; in *Hamlet,* the cause of Hamlet's death.

APPROPRIATE USE

■ To analyze literature story lines, sociological problems, historic events, current events, geological catastrophes, business successes, environmental changes, etc.

■ To predict a *most likely* cause in a complicated situation.

NAME _____   CLASS _____

THE FISH BONE

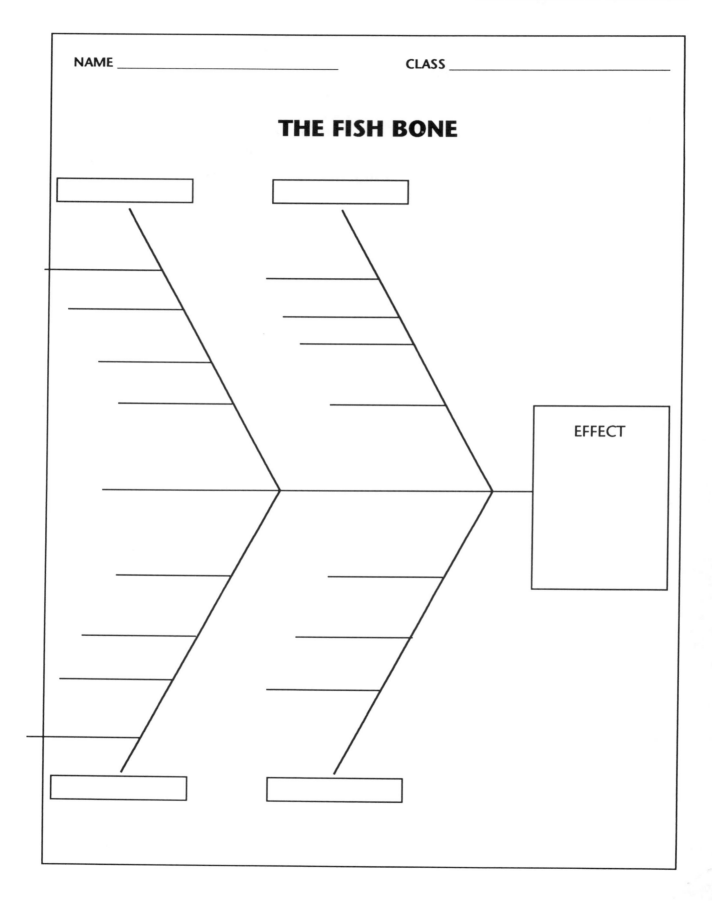

EFFECT

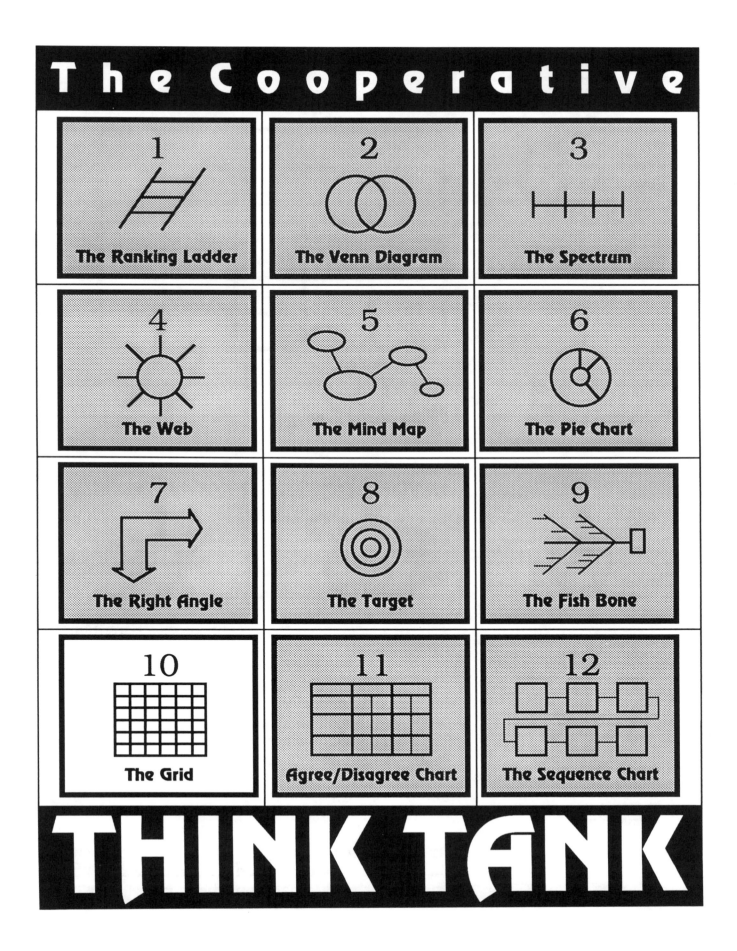

C H A P T E R

10

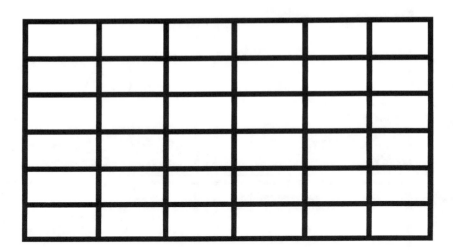

The Grid

INTRODUCTORY LESSON

Draw a grid on the board or show pictures of the grid on your overhead screen. Ask students to tell you about grids that they know (grid iron or football field, math grids, database software grids, etc.) and what those grids have in common.

Tell the class about the creator of the "Lone Ranger" radio and television story. Each week he had to write a new story with the same characters: a masked man who rode a white horse named "Silver" and shot outlaws with silver bullets as he tried to bring law and order to the wild west; a faithful Indian companion, Tonto; assorted outlaws and criminals; and an ending in which the Lone Ranger and Tonto rode away while the townspeople asked "who was that masked man?" and hearing the Lone Ranger shout out "hi-ho Silver, away."

To help himself come up with a new story every week, the writer invented the word grid. Use the sample grid on the overhead to point out the model.

■ PURPOSE

To help students make creative combinations.

■ VOCABULARY

Brainstorm: To generate unjudged lists of ideas.

Conflict: A disagreement or fight between two or more persons. The conflict can be about facts, ideas, goals, values or beliefs.

Setting: The place or location in which a story takes place.

Ending: The final events in a story.

■ THINKING SKILL

Brainstorming

The Lone Ranger Model

Good guy	Sidekick	Bad guy	Gal	Conflict	Setting	Ending
doctor	Indian	city slicker	floosie	man vs. nature	1800's	cliff hanger
lawyer	bum	land baron	dance hall girl	robbery	closet	everyone happy
Indian chief	deputy	bully	school teacher	town vs. stranger	Montana	serial
marshall	relative	ex-con	widow	large bank deposit lost	town	tragic
stranger	friend	gambler	miner's daughter	man vs. self	desert	butler did it
bartender	foreigner	politician	eastern cousin	good vs. evil	saloon	boy marries girl
shop owner	town drunk	lawyer	wife	family wins a million dollars	mountain	bad guy is transformed
preacher	little kid	bank clerk	old sweetheart	train stuck on cliff	town hall	everyone dies
uncle	a bear	little kid	tomboy	ranchers vs. disease	livery stable	bad guy wins
wife	ex-con	gang member	little sister	cowboys vs. Indians	main street	stranger becomes sheriff

Ask the students to think of their favorite TV or comic strip stories. Fill in some samples on a blank grid. Explain any heading not understood (e.g., setting). As you model putting answers in columns, check to see that each answer volunteered is first agreed to by all the students before you write it on the grid. It is OK to write an answer in more than one column if all agree.

Divide the class into groups of four. Assign the roles of checker, recorder, encourager, and materials gopher. The gopher gets the materials for the task—newsprint, markers and tape—and ensures that the quiet rules are followed. Review the roles, especially the checker

AN ELEMENTARY SCHOOL SAMPLE

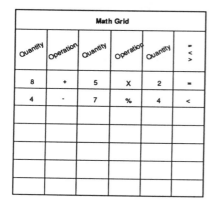

Math Grid

Quantity	Operation	Quantity	Operation	Quantity	= < >
8	+	5	X	2	=
4	-	7	%	4	<

A MIDDLE SCHOOL SAMPLE

Grammar Grid

Adverbs	Verbs	Adjectives	Nouns	Prepositions	Conjunctions
Happily	Running	White	Window	Over	But
Very	Buying	Unique	Cow	From	However

who will have to make sure everyone agrees on which words go into which column. Review the DOVE guidelines and insist that groups follow them. Let them know that you will be observing and evaluating how well they use the guidelines in the task.

Invite the gophers to get two sheets of newsprint. (If you don't have newsprint, use 8 1/2 x 11 paper with the grid duplicated on it.) The recorder can sketch out the grid and enter the headings. Remind the recorder to use the full size so when the group is asked to present everyone can see. Another option, if you don't have newsprint, is to duplicate the blank grid on six or seven transparencies and let the recorders use washable pen to record on the masters. When they are asked to do the presentations, they can work right on the overhead.

Ask the checkers to check instructions with the group. You may wish to follow this with a random check of any group member to ensure everyone knows what to do before the task starts. Allow 10 minutes for each group to brainstorm (remember DOVE) names for each column. Insist that the groups complete one column at a time. Suggest that they cover up completed columns so association in each column stays clean of a story they know. They can use names from stories they know, history, current events, TV, movies, etc. The one thing they cannot do is use names of people they know such as parents, friends, kids in school, teachers, family members, etc. Encourage wild abandon and randomness.

At the end of the 10 minutes or when most of the groups are finished, stop the task. Ask one class member to tell his/her home phone number (or use some other random number selection). Use the numbers to circle a word in each column. For instance, if the seven numbers are 9163200, your completed model would look like the example on the next page. (Note that 0 = 10.)

Give each group a random code to circle its words.

After the recorders have done this step, ask for some volunteers to identify the column head and the word randomly chosen from each heading.

Using your model, demonstrate how to write a two- to three- sentence story line using the circled information. For example, the above story line might start like this:

Uncle Festus has a showdown with the crooked politician who robbed the townspeople of the...

The Lone Ranger Model

Good guy	Sidekick	Bad guy	Gal	Conflict	Setting	Ending
doctor	Indian	city slicker	floosie	man vs. nature	1800's	cliff hanger
lawyer	old miner	land baron	dance hall girl	robbery	closet	everyone happy
Indian chief	deputy	bully	school teacher	town vs. stranger	Montana	serial
marshall	relative	ex-con	widow	husband vs. wife	town	tragic
stranger	friend	gambler	miner's daughter	man vs. self	desert	butler did it
bartender	foreigner	politician	eastern cousin	good vs. evil	saloon	boy marries girl
shop owner	town drunk	lawyer	wife	cattlemen vs. farmers	mountain	bad guy is transformed
preacher	little kid	bank clerk	old sweetheart	town vs. railroad	town hall	everyone dies
uncle	a bear	little kid	tomboy	ranchers vs. disease	livery stable	bad guy wins
wife	ex-con	gang member	little sister	cowboys vs. Indians	main street	stranger becomes sheriff

A SECONDARY SCHOOL SAMPLE

Sewing Grid					
Fabric	Neckline	Sleeve	Fasteners	Color	Hemline
Cotton	Jewel	Long	Zipper	Red	Short
Nylon	V-neck	Cuff	Buttons	Yellow	Mid-calf

Instruct the groups to take the next five minutes to create a story line from the words they selected in their grids. After the group has agreed on its story line (no more than three sentences), instruct the recorder to write it out in large letters on the second sheet of newsprint, overhead or blackline master. Have each group review the result and edit for punctuation, grammar and sentence correctness. Circulate and give help as needed.

When the editing is complete, invite each group to share its sheets with the class. Every member of each group is expected to say something in the presentation. Invite the class to applaud each presentation.

REVIEW & TRANSFER

Ask the students to tell why the DOVE guidelines were so important to successful completion of the task (no put-downs, no making fun, everyone contributes, it's OK to have a very different idea, etc.).

Assign groups of three to complete a new grid. List the key steps on the board or overhead.

1. Assign roles and review DOVE.
2. Pick a random number to use.
3. Brainstorm by column.
4. Circle words.
5. Write your story line.
6. Evaluate your group work and turn in all work.

Set a time limit for the entire task.

YOUR IDEA FOR A GRID

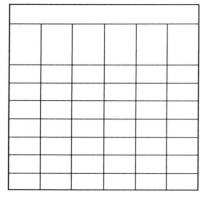

After you have reviewed the story lines for each group, you may want the groups to flush out or expand on the stories in one or two pages or a mini book with pictures. Be sure to structure positive interdependence. For instance, the new group roles might include editor, illustrator, writer.

After you used this grid model several times in the classroom and students see how to use it for writing short stories, you can expand it for use in writing a longer TV script, a comic strip, longer short stories or some other creative writing task.

The grid lends itself well for helping students transfer a thinking and learning tool across the curriculum. Pick a different subject area such as geography, biology, geometry, business or P.E. Construct a grid and provide the headings as ingredients in a creative task in that area. For instance, in math the headings may be the ingredients in a word problem; in science, the steps of the scientific process (you provide the number of columns that fit the task); in P.E., the ingredients for a game.

As students become more experienced with the grid as a pre-writing tool or as a way to understand and link the key processes in a content area, add more sophisticated questions that help them plan, monitor and evaluate their thinking.

TEST

To test students' mastery of the grid as a learning and thinking tool:

- ☐ Using the multiple choice format or fill-in-the-blanks, have students explain in their own words *grid, brainstorming, DOVE, setting, conflict,* and *ending.*
- ☐ Provide the students with the basic grid as used in the Lone Ranger model. Instruct them to write a set of instructions to a class of students who do not know how to use it.

OPTIONAL

For more advanced practice, have students use grids to develop a series of essays, short stories or word problems. After the students have made the grids and composed the outlines or problems, rotate the grids for another group to write the story. Also use the grid to initiate a play outline, then have the students write and perform the plays.

APPROPRIATE USE

■ To generate complex ideas for a story, word problem, process guidelines, or historic situation.

■ To help students understand the basic creative structure of a task or problem inherent in an academic discipline.

■ To generate and organize concepts as a pre-writing tool.

NAME _____   CLASS _____

THE GRID

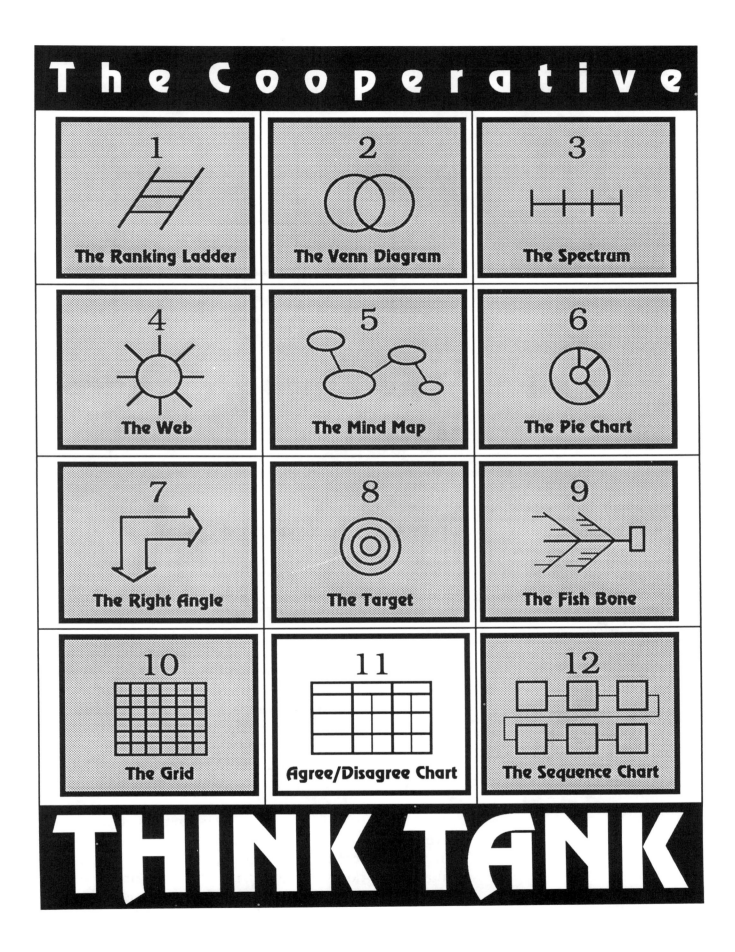

CHAPTER

11

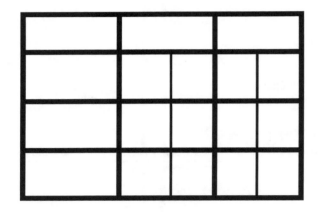

The Agree/Disagree Chart

■ **PURPOSE**

To help students organize data to support a position for or against an idea.

■ **VOCABULARY**

Agree: To be in favor of an idea.

Disagree: To be against an idea.

■ **THINKING SKILLS**

Evaluating, analyzing

INTRODUCTORY LESSON

On the board or overhead, write this statement:

> *The bigger you are, the more alcohol you can drink before getting drunk.*

Ask for volunteers to agree or disagree with the statement and to give you a reason. After you have several reasons for and against the statement, ask the students to move. All the students who agree with the idea stand on the right side of the room. All who disagree with the idea stand on the left side of the room. Each group will pick out the most important reason for the position and share it with the class.

After the students are reseated, show the chart on the overhead. Point out that skillful thinkers will always think about the arguments for both sides before making a decision and that they might very well change what they think based on the data they collect.

Charlotte's Web	Before		After	
	Agree	Disagree	Agree	Disagree
1. Spiders are a nuisance.				
2. Spiders are scary.				
3. Spiders have no feelings.				
4.				
5.				

Here is a sample from E.B. White's *Charlotte's Web.*

For each of the following statements, ask each student who agrees with the idea to give a thumbs-up signal. Count the numbers and record on the agree/disagree chart. For all who disagree with each statement, get a thumbs-down count and record it on the agree/disagree chart.

Spiders are a nuisance.
Spiders are scary.
Spiders have no feelings.

Assign students to read the story. When all are finished, do a recount and record on the chart. Discuss with the class why the counts were different. (You may wish to select a story more appropriate to your students' ages, abilities, and interests.)

Next, divide the students into groups of three, with a recorder, reader, and a checker/encourager.

**A SECONDARY
SCHOOL SAMPLE**

Alcohol	Before		After	
	A	D	A	D
1. Black coffee will sober you up.				
2. There is an equal amount of alcohol in a glass of wine and a glass of beer.				
3. Spiders have no feelings.				

**CREATE YOUR OWN
AGREE/DISAGREE CHART**

	Before		After	
	A	D	A	D
1.				
2.				
3.				

Review the roles and guidelines. Using the blank chart, add statements for the story you have selected. Instruct each group to vote on the results. Have the reader read the story. When finished, the group will re-vote and re-tally its ideas. On the back of the sheet, the group must agree on no more than three reasons why each change in the vote occurred. All members must be ready to explain these reasons.

Conclude the activity by inviting several groups to explain the differences and for the class to discuss the major reasons given.

REVIEW & TRANSFER

Review with the class the major steps in the agree-disagree process. Discuss why it is helpful to use the chart and brainstorm other places or times they might use the chart inside and outside of school. Seek many different uses and record each. Make an agree/disagree chart for the ideas provided and ask the groups to agree on their ideas as they did in the introductory lesson.

Throughout the next unit, use the chart to promote student thinking about your content. Give refinement and feedback on the students' uses of the chart. Look for more thorough reasons for changes. End the unit with an individualized task in which each student completes a chart you made for a selected story.

TEST

To test student facility with the agree/disagree chart and students' ability to give reasons for changes in thinking:

☐ Ask each student to explain why it is important to use the chart to organize and track ideas before and after studying an idea.

☐ Ask each student to complete a chart that you make and to come up with appropriate reasons for the changes.

☐ Ask each student to write instructions for use of a chart that you supply.

☐ Ask each student to take a brief story, a current editorial or information about a current issue and construct a chart with instructions for its completion.

OPTIONAL

Adapt this chart to the difficulty of the reading material in your class—i.e., emphasize different points of view, cut editorials from the current newspaper or select controversial articles. Follow up the agree/disagree analysis with assignments for debates or editorials.

APPROPRIATE USE

■ To evaluate issues, readings and ideas that will be subject to revised opinion when information is provided.

■ To emphasize points of view and the effects of biased or "swayed" information.

NAME _____   CLASS _____

THE AGREE/DISAGREE CHART

Statement	Before		After	
	Agree	Disagree	Agree	Disagree
1				
2				
3				
4				
5				
6				
7				
8				
9				
10				

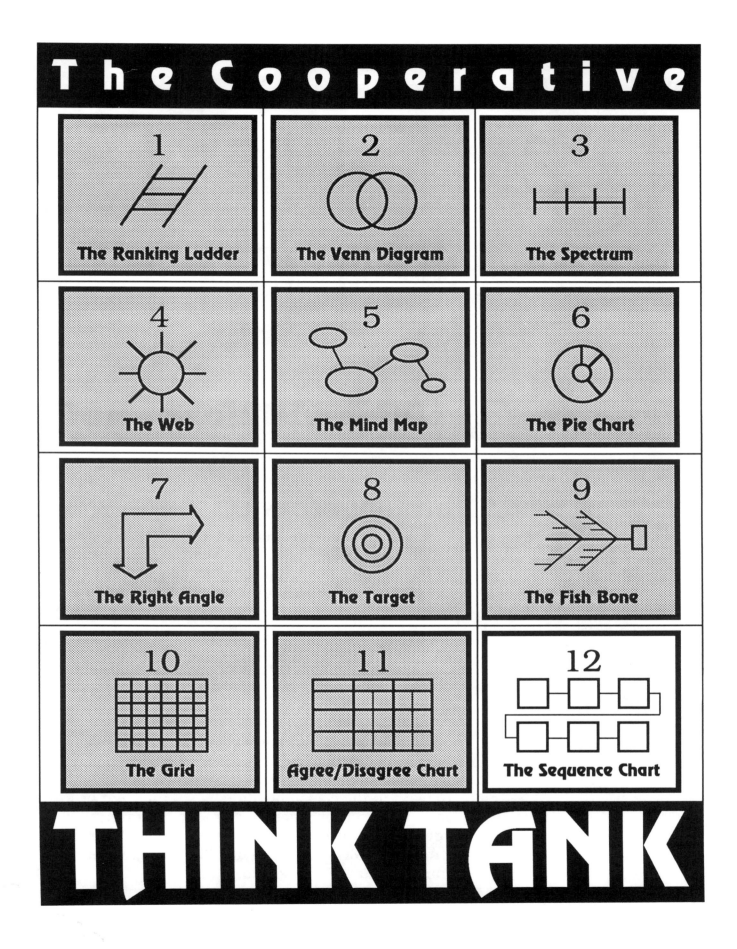

CHAPTER

12

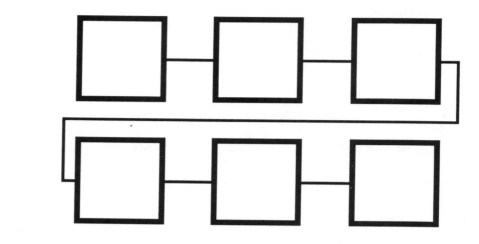

The Sequence Chart

■ **PURPOSE**

To help students sequence a series of actions or tasks chronologically.

■ **VOCABULARY**

Sequence: To put into order.

Problem: A block or barrier to achieving a goal or desired result.

■ **THINKING SKILLS**

Problem solving, sequencing

INTRODUCTORY LESSON

On the blackboard or overhead list the following years: 1492, 1941, 1776, 1865, this year. Ask the students to put the dates in a time or chronological order from the earliest to the most current. After the dates are in the correct order, ask students to identify a major event associated with each date.

1492	discovery of America by Columbus
1776	signing of the Declaration of Independence
1865	end of the Civil War
1941	beginning of World War II
_____	attending this class

Explain to the class how time (when an event occurs) sets up an order called a sequence of events. It is important to learn how to sequence events or tasks chronologically when studying literature, history, science and almost every field.

On the board or overhead show the sequence chart. Tell the class that they will work with this chart to help them see how events are arranged chronologically in a story.

Next, tell a familiar story such as "The Three Bears," "The Billy Goats Gruff" or "The Three Little Pigs." (Use the same stories for older children, but preface it by telling students you selected a simple story as an example.) Ask a volunteer to tell you the problem in the story.

PROBLEM The billy goats wanted to eat the grass on the other side of the bridge, but the troll was going to eat them if they tried to cross it.

Next, ask the class to brainstorm as many events as possible that occurred in the story. Record the responses on the board (listing the items randomly, not in chronological order). You may want to provide the list for very young students.

EVENTS
baby goat goes across
big goat goes across
goats decide to cross the bridge
baby goat gets to green grass
troll stops baby goat
etc.

**AN ELEMENTARY
SCHOOL SAMPLE**

To find a book

**A MIDDLE
SCHOOL SAMPLE**

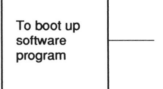

SEQUENCE

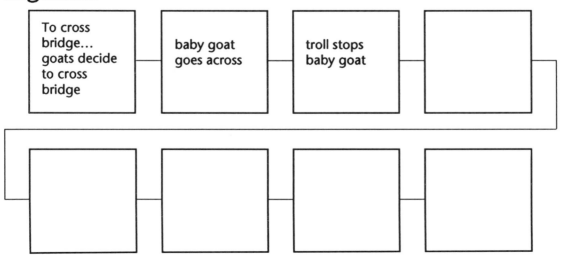

Ask the class to help you put the events in sequence in the sequence boxes, one event per box.

After the class agrees that all the major events are in the right order, divide the class into groups of three. Assign a recorder, reader, and checker/encourager to each group. Distribute a sequence chart to each group. On the board or overhead, list in order the steps for each group to follow:

1. Read your story and identify a problem faced by the main character. Draw a picture of the problem on the sequence chart.

2. Pick out the eight most important events that lead to the solution of the problem. Draw a picture of each event in the correct box.

3. Use no more than two or three words to label each box.

You may want all students to work with the same story or you might give each group a different story to sequence.

After each group is finished, the checker should make sure that each member of the group can explain its chart. Select several different groups to explain their charts. Complete the lesson by asking students to write one thing they learned about sequencing. The recorders write the responses on the back of the chart and obtain signatures from each of the contributors.

REVIEW & TRANSFER

Select other stories which groups can use for practice. You may want to use news articles, magazine stories, TV shows, biographies, historic events, etc. for students to practice the skill of sequencing as you introduce new content. After you determine that students have learned how to sequence in group work, assign each student an individual reading task and the sequence chart. If you have students do daily silent reading in class, invite them to turn in a sequence chart for each book completed.

TEST

To test students' knowledge of sequences:

- ☐ Ask each student to explain the terms *sequence* and *problem* in his/her own words and to provide an example of each from his/her daily routine.

- ☐ Give each student a list of events that might occur in the school week or year. Instruct each student to sequence the events.

- ☐ Give each student a short reading that describes steps in completing a common task. Instruct each student to complete a sequence chart for task/problem.

- ☐ Instruct each student to construct a sequence chart and to write instructions for its use.

OPTIONAL

For advanced practice, provide students with a packet of sequence charts to use with the reading of a novel.

For younger students, cut several days worth of a comic from the newspaper and mix up the frames. Instruct the groups to put the frames in order and glue them to the chart.

For a creative task, invite the student groups to create their own comic strips. After they select a problem, they can brainstorm the actions and events and use the chart to create the sequence.

In social studies, use the charts with events watched as a video.

In science, use the charts to sequence tasks as an experiment.

APPROPRIATE USE

- ■ To organize any classroom task that has sequences of activities (lab experiments, stories, procedures, etc.).
- ■ To break down a complex sequence.
- ■ To chart a seemingly random process or event.

A SECONDARY SCHOOL SAMPLE

To prove
a theorem

YOUR IDEA FOR THE SEQUENCING

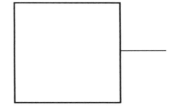

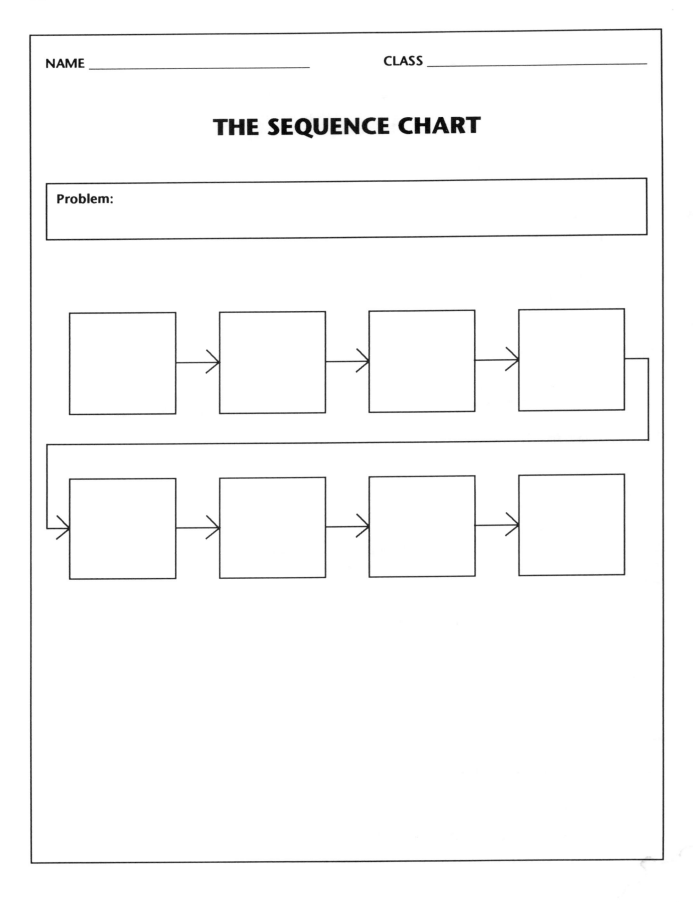

NAME _____   CLASS _____

THE SEQUENCE CHART

Problem:

BIBLIOGRAPHY

Bellanca, J. (1992). *The cooperative think tank II: Graphic organizers to teach thinking in the cooperative classroom.* Palatine, IL: Skylight Publishing.

Berliner, D. (1986). Use what kids know to teach the new. *Instructor, 95,* 12–13.

Black, H., & Black, S. (1990). *Organizing thinking: Graphic organizers* (Book II). Pacific Grove, CA: Critical Thinking Press & Software.

Brown, A. (1980). Metacognitive development and reading. In P. Spriro, B. Bruce, & W. Brewer (Eds.), *Theoretical issues in reading comprehension.* Hillsdale, NJ: Erlbaum.

Brown, A., Campione, J., & Day, J. (1981). Learning to learn: On training students to learn from texts. *Educational Researcher, 10.*

Brown, A., & Palincsar, A. (1982). Inducing strategic learning from texts by means of informed, self-control training. *Topics in Learning and Learning Disabilities, 2.*

Buzan, T. (1984). *Make the most of your mind.* New York: Simon & Schuster.

de Bono, E. (1983). The direct teaching of thinking as a skill. *Phi Delta Kappan, 64*(1), 703–708.

Deming, E. (1986). *Out of the crisis.* Cambridge, MA: MIT Center for Advanced Engineering Study.

Fogarty, R., & Bellanca, J. (1991). *Patterns for thinking: Patterns for transfer.* Palatine, IL: Skylight Publishing.

Hawley, R. (1976). *Evaluating teaching: A handbook of positive approaches.* Amherst, MA: Education Research Associates.

Jones, B. F., Palincsar, A. S., Ogle, D. S., & Carr, E. G. (Eds.). (1987). *Strategic teaching and learning: Cognitive instruction in the content areas.* Alexandria, VA: Association for Supervision and Curriculum Development.

Jones, B. F., Pierce, J., & Hunter, B. (1988). Teaching students to construct graphic representations. *Educational Leadership, 46.*

Jones, B. F., Pierce, J., & Hunter, B. (1988). *Using graphic representations as a strategy for analysis and problem solving.* Paper submitted to the Association for Supervision and Curriculum Development, Alexandria, VA.

McTighe, J., & Lyman, F. (1992). Mind tools for matters of the mind. In A. Costa, J. Bellanca, & R. Fogarty (Eds.), *If minds matter: A foreword to the future* (Vol. II). Palatine, IL: Skylight Publishing.

Ogle, D. (1986). K-W-L group instruction strategy. In A. Palincsar, D. Ogle, B. Jones, & E. Carr (Eds.), *Teaching techniques as thinking (Teleconference resource guide)*. Alexandria, VA: Association for Supervision and Curriculum Development.

Palincsar, A. S., & Brown, A. L. (1985). Reciprocal teaching: Activities to promote reading with your mind. In T. L. Harris & E. J. Cogen (Eds.), *Reading, thinking, and concept development: Strategies for the classroom.* New York: College Board.

Pearson, P. D., Hansen, J., & Gordon, C. (1979). The effect of background knowledge on young children's comprehension of explicit and implicit information. *Journal of Reading Behavior, 11*, 201–209.

Rico, G. (1983). *Writing the natural way: Using right-brain techniques to release your expressive powers.* Los Angeles: Tarcher.

Senge, P. (1990). *The fifth discipline: The arts and practice of the learning organization.* New York: Doubleday.

Vacca, J. L. (1986). Working with content area teachers. In R. T. Vacca & J. L. Vacca (Eds.), *Content area reading.* Boston: Little, Brown.

Vacca, R. T., & Vacca, J. L. (1986). *Content area reading* (2nd ed.). Boston: Little, Brown.

Vygotsky, L. S. (1978). *Mind in society: The development of higher psychological processes.* Cambridge, MA: Harvard University Press.

Training and Publishing Inc.

We Prepare Your Teachers Today
for the Classrooms of Tomorrow

Learn from Our Books and from Our Authors!

Ignite Learning in Your School or District.

SkyLight's team of classroom-experienced consultants can help you foster systemic change for increased student achievement.

Professional development is a process, not an event. SkyLight's seasoned practitioners drive the creation of our on-site professional development programs, graduate courses, research-based publications, interactive video courses, teacher-friendly training materials, and online resources—call SkyLight Training and Publishing Inc. today.

SkyLight specializes in three professional development areas.

Specialty # **1** **Best Practices**

We **model** the best practices that result in improved student performance and guided applications.

Specialty # **2** **Making the Innovations Last**

We help set up **support** systems that make innovations part of everyday practice in the long-term systemic improvement of your school or district.

Specialty # **3** **How to Assess the Results**

We prepare your school leaders to encourage and **assess** teacher growth, **measure** student achievement, and **evaluate** program success.

Contact the SkyLight team and begin a process toward long-term results.

Training and Publishing Inc.

2626 S. Clearbrook Dr., Arlington Heights, IL 60005
800-348-4474 • 847-290-6600 • FAX 847-290-6609
http://www.iriskylight.com

There are

one-story intellects,

two-story intellects, and three-story

intellects with skylights. All fact collectors, who

have no aim beyond their facts, are one-story men. Two-story men

compare, reason, generalize, using the labors of the fact collectors as

well as their own. Three-story men idealize, imagine,

predict—their best illumination comes from

above, through the skylight.

—*Oliver Wendell*

Holmes

Training and Publishing Inc.